D1411692

CASUAL LEX

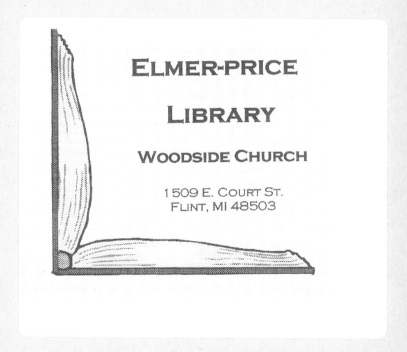

ELMER-PRICE

LIBRARY

WOODSIDE CHURCH

1509 E. COURT ST.
FLINT, MI 48503

CASUAL LEX

An Informal Assemblage of Why We Say What We Say

WEBB GARRISON

RUTLEDGE HILL PRESS
Nashville, Tennessee
A Division of Thomas Nelson Publishers
Since 1798

www.thomasnelson.com

Copyright © 2005 by Bill Garrison, Webb Garrison Jr., and Carol Bates.

This book is compiled and updated from material originally published in *Why You Say It*, copyright © 1992 by Webb Garrison, and *What's in a Word?*, copyright © 2000 by Webb Garrison, both published by Rutledge Hill Press.

All rights reserved. No portion of this book may be reproduced, stored in a retrieval system, or transmitted in any form or by any means—electronic, mechanical, photocopy, recording, or any other—except for brief quotations in printed reviews, without prior permission of the publisher.

Published by Rutledge Hill Press, a Division of Thomas Nelson, Inc., P.O. Box 141000, Nashville, Tennessee 37214.

Rutledge Hill Press books may be purchased in bulk for educational, business, fundraising, or sales promotional use. For information, please e-mail SpecialMarkets@ThomasNelson.com.

Library of Congress Cataloging-in-Publication Data

Garrison, Webb B.
    Casual lex : an informal assemblage of why we say what we say / Webb Garrison.
      p. cm.
    "This book is compiled and updated from material originally published in Why you say it . . . and . . . What's in a word? . . . by Webb Garrison."
    Includes bibliographical references.
    ISBN 1-4016-0218-5 (pbk.)
    1. English language—Etymology—Dictionaries. 2. English language—Idioms—Dictionaries. 3. English language—Terms and phrases. I. Garrison, Webb B. Why you say it. II. Garrison, Webb B. What's in a word? III. Title.
PE1580.G367 2005
422'.03—dc22   2005000837

Printed in the United States of America

05 06 07 08 09 RRD 5 4 3 2 1

FOREWORD

Growing up with Webb Garrison as our father, we rarely had a meal when the dictionary was not consulted. We used it to resolve family arguments on word usage or etymology. One of our Dad's prized possessions was the unabridged *Webster's* that resided on a special table. It was not a fancy table, but it was treated almost like an altar. We were allowed to touch it and use it but not to remove it from its resting place.

Our father, the author of the original two books that were combined and abridged to make this new edition, loved working with words. So he set out to compile and catalog the history of everyday speech, eventually putting together a collection of hundreds of words and phrases used in common parlance. He wanted to share with readers the colorful background behind words such as *bikini, diddly-squat,* and *fiasco.* These words and their intriguing stories are part of the fun of our uniquely American speech.

When Dad was performing his research for what has now become *Casual Lex,* he went to numerous scholarly works, most notably the 22,000-page *Oxford English Dictionary,* which includes detailed accounts of the way speech has developed. He found such references cumbersome and out of touch with how people really speak in everyday life. He provided an alternative approach to the history of words, explaining their fascinating origins through amusing, breezy entries.

Casual Lex is a collection of concise explanations of expressions in wide use. Included are many words and phrases not even in use fifty years ago when the original version of this book, then titled *Why You Say It,* was published by Abingdon Press (1955). Over the years, in a revised edition of *Why You Say It* (Rutledge Hill Press, 1992) and in a second volume, *What's in a Word?* (Rutledge Hill Press, 2000), our father has updated his lexicon to include newly coined words such as *spam* and *hacker*, as well as terms once considered taboo in polite circles, such as *prostitute* and *condom*. Our casual lexicon is an ever-changing organism, with new phrases and terms becoming part of our speech almost every day. Although many terms remain popular for years, a good portion of what was familiar twenty or thirty years ago is rarely heard today. A few of these almost obsolete terms, such as *rhubarb* and *screaming meemies*, are included in this new edition because their stories are so interesting. Consider those aged entries a retro look at what folks used to say and why they said it.

Dad was especially well suited to writing about language. Many readers knew him primarily as a prolific Civil War author, but Dad also relished the craft of writing, massaging the words to create his own special style of literary expression. He had his own unique voice, and he was a master of the anecdotal gem. Nothing pleased him more than when the opportunity presented itself for him to interject some fascinating anecdote or another. And it is these stories that are at the heart of *Casual Lex*.

Our father passed away a few years ago, but we hope this new work will help keep his love for the written word alive for years to come. It would give him great joy to know that you'll have fun discovering why you say some of the things that mark you as an individual, using inherited words and phrases in a fashion unique to you.

— Carol Bates, Webb Garrison Jr.,
and William Garrison,
the children of Webb Garrison

CASUAL LEX

ABOVEBOARD

Gamblers and confidence men have followed the track since the beginning of organized horse racing. A standard attraction at a medieval race was a crude gambling wheel that was a forerunner of the roulette wheel we know today. This device was customarily mounted on a stand, the sides of which were draped with brightly colored cloth.

Unscrupulous operators would install a treadle under the stand to regulate the stopping point of the wheel. Though the ruse was exposed, it continued to flourish. A gambler who wished to convince bystanders of the honesty of his game would point to his wheel and cry, "All above the board, sirs! All above the board!" This claim that there was no concealed treadle under the board soon entered common speech as *aboveboard*, meaning "straightforward" or "without concealment."

ACE IN THE HOLE

Stud poker was popularized during the cowboy era. More than any other game, it separated cowpokes from their wages and miners from their dust. Complex rules govern the way in which cards are dealt, held, and played.

With other cards exposed so that opponents may see them, a lucky player sometimes holds an ace that is face down—concealed "in the hole." That card may be the pivot on which a game turns.

Any asset or source of strength, kept secret by its holder, is so much like a concealed playing card that it is an *ace in the hole*.

ACHILLES' HEEL

Regardless of how tough a person may be, he or she has a weak spot somewhere. Such was the case with one of the greatest heroes of Greek mythology.

In ancient times it was common knowledge that the water of the river Styx was potent—so potent that a baby dipped into it received supernatural protection. Skin touched by the water remained pliable yet tough as steel.

One mother decided to give her son a kind of immortality. Hours after the boy was delivered, she hurried to the river and, holding him by his heel, dipped him into the mysterious water. That made Achilles invulnerable over most of his body.

But in the end, Achilles was killed during the Trojan War by a wound to his heel—the part left covered when his mother dipped him in the river. Water didn't touch his heel, so the mythological superman had a small but mortal flaw.

Stories about the mother's son have survived after many centuries. As a result, any seemingly invincible person's weakest point is his or her *Achilles' heel.*

ACID TEST

Wandering peddlers, who have since given way to telemarketers, were once a familiar part of the European and American scene. A typical fellow carried a few household articles in a pack; if well established, he might drive a wagon with a variety of goods.

Many a peddler made his real money not by the sale of goods but by the purchase of old gold from persons he encountered. Even a veteran found it hard to assess the value of filled and plated articles by examination. But a positive test was easily used. After filing a shallow groove in a piece, the prospective buyer would touch it with nitric acid. Color reactions gave a reasonably accurate index as to the gold content and hence the true value.

Bottles of nitric acid were used on so many articles containing gold that any exacting trial came to be called an *acid test.*

ADAM'S APPLE

Count Abraham Lincoln among the famous people sporting a prominent *Adam's apple*. Male chauvinism is responsible for the centuries-old name.

Pioneer English anatomists were puzzled by the section of cartilage that refused to stay in one spot. Folktales explained that Adam should not have taken that apple from Eve in the Garden of Eden. When he yielded to her temptation, a piece of fruit stuck on the way down. Ever since, it has moved when men eat or talk in order to warn: "Beware of the temptress!"

In truth, the growth of the visible knot is stimulated by male hormones. Because women have a small amount of this hormone, they also have a small version of the *Adam's apple*.

ALCOHOL

Antimony is a mineral common in Egypt and the Middle East. Arabs made a fine black powder with the antimony and called it *kohl*. Dabbed onto the eyelids, the stain was one of the earliest cosmetics.

Queens and women of wealth spent fortunes on the finest variety of eye shadow, which they called *al-kohl*—literally "the powder." Queen Shub-ad of Ur kept her al-kohl in a silver box fifty-five hundred years ago.

By the early seventeenth century, western travelers used *alcohol* for "fine powder that stains." Eventually it referred to any substance obtained from an essence—and particularly distillation. Thus *alcohol of wine* meant the "essence of wine." Soon it became simply *alcohol*; thus, today's liquid refreshments bear the name of eye shadow used by beauties of ancient Egypt.

ALIAS

Scholars of medieval England developed great pride in their learning. A "man of letters" seldom used ordinary language. Instead he relied almost entirely upon Latin.

Lawyers fond of displaying their knowledge frequently used Latin phrases, even in their courtroom addresses. One such expression was *alias dictus*, meaning "otherwise called." A criminal known by more than one name might be mentioned as Richard Stone, *alias dictus* Robert Scott. Use of the sonorous phrase was so frequent that by 1535 ordinary folk had adopted the word *alias* to designate any assumed name.

ALIBI

Courtroom practices are slow to change. Lawyers continued to use Latin long after it was abandoned in everyday speech.

Alibi was a Latin term meaning "elsewhere" and for centuries was standard in criminal cases. It was common for a defense attorney to rest his case upon evidence that his client was *alibi* at the time of the crime.

Use of the centuries-old term was so common that it entered modern speech with no change in spelling and little difference in meaning. An accused person who is able to establish an *alibi* is almost like a citizen in the realm of the Caesars who answered an accusation by saying he or she was elsewhere when the deed was done.

ALL OVER BUT THE SHOUTING

Until modern times, adult white males who paid taxes or could provide military service were the only citizens allowed to vote. Election day was set aside for talking, drinking, and carousing after having voted.

Ballots were hand counted, so results were not announced until long after the polls had closed. Especially in a tight election, announcement of the count was likely to trigger a roar from supporters of the winning candidate.

In a one-sided contest, everybody knew the winner long before the last ballot was counted. This meant that when the polls closed, the outcome was unofficial but decided—it was *all over but the shouting* of victory.

ALLERGY

Late in the nineteenth century, physicians developed great interest in a puzzling phenomenon. Patients who were helped by the first dose of a new drug sometimes had adverse reactions to later doses. At a loss for a more precise name, specialists used the Greek word *allos* (other) to coin the word *allergy*, a condition in which reactions are other than standard.

By 1925 the new word had come into general medical use to refer to the peculiar reactions a person has to a variety of substances, whether they be foods, drugs, or environmental elements such as pollen.

ALSO-RAN

In many horse races, only the first three animals to cross the line are counted. Others in the field follow, but the order in which they finish may not be announced.

Newspapers of the nineteenth century made readers familiar with animals that placed in major races. All three were frequently described, with their times, owners, and winnings listed. Toward the end of such a story, it was a common practice to mention many or all of the horses that also ran.

Presidential elections came more and more to resemble horse races with crowded fields. In reporting results of an election, newspapers dismissed many an aspirant for the White House as an *also-ran*—one who was so far back in the field that his finish order wasn't computed.

By the turn of the century, the political term borrowed from the racetrack was being applied to a person badly beaten in any competition.

APOCALYPTIC

Ancient Greek housewives employed special cloths to keep dust out of food pots. They even devised a technical word meaning "to take away the cover." Romans who borrowed the term from these housewives modified it to *apocalypsis*.

By 200 BC, Judea was in a state of turmoil that lasted for three centuries. National and international distress helped produce a stream of literature making predictions about the future. Hope of sharing in the future glory of God's kingdom made it somewhat easier to bear the burdens of the age. Since a document of this type helped "take away the cover" from the future, Jews called it an *apocalypse*.

Though many apocalypses were produced, only one stood the test of time: the stirring and poetic account of John's visions on the island of Patmos. Today it is referred to as "the Revelation of Saint John," but to the early church it was known as "the Apocalypse." The impact of this dynamic document was so great that any vision or prophecy dealing with the coming of God's earthly reign is termed *apocalyptic* literature.

ASSEMBLY LINE JOB

Mass production of cars was late in starting. Henry Ford got the idea from watching an overhead trolley in a Chicago packing plant. In order to build automobiles in large quantity, he had Model-T flywheel magnetos move slowly past workers who each performed only one or two operations.

Production soared 400 percent, so he moved from magnetos to

engines and transmissions and then to complete cars. Model-T's in the making, conveyed at six feet per minute past workers who used standardized parts, were sold at prices not imagined when cars were handmade luxuries. Ford launched modern mass production, yet the workers soon complained that their jobs were monotonous.

Even when performed at the keyboard of a computer instead of beside a conveyor belt, any highly repetitive work is likely to be criticized as an *assembly line job*.

AT LOOSE ENDS

During the days of the windjammers and other great sailing vessels, rigging grew more and more complex. On many ships there were literally hundreds of ropes. If these ropes had been left free to ravel, a hopeless tangle could have resulted. So every ship's master prided himself on the good condition of his "ends"—the taped ends of his ropes.

When other work was slack, members of the crew were frequently put to work repairing the loose ends. Many a captain was accused of ordering such work to keep his men occupied, so a person with nothing important to do is said to be *at loose ends*.

AT THE DROP OF A HAT

Dueling by prescribed rules was common in the United States until the mid-1800s, although the various states began to outlaw it, beginning with Tennessee in 1801. In one of the most famous duels, Aaron Burr, the vice president of the United States, killed Alexander Hamilton, former secretary of the treasury.

According to the dueling code, the man challenged had the choice of weapons, and usually they were pistols in America. Each duelist chose a friend to act as a "second," and a surgeon often attended. To avoid the law officers, the meetings often took place at dawn in a forest clearing. The duelists stood back to back and marched an agreed number of paces in opposite directions. Then one of the seconds dropped a handkerchief, and the fighters turned and fired.

On the frontier, disagreements were settled much more informally. Participants used guns, knives, whips, or fists—and they often fought in broad daylight before an audience. The referee would drop a hat (often more readily available than a handkerchief) to start the fight.

The phrase *at the drop of a hat*, meaning ready to begin a fight or other undertaking, apparently was first used in the West around 1887.

AWOL

These days, it's possible for one of your fellow workers to go *AWOL,* or walk off the job without giving notice. Earlier, reference to this term was limited to members of the military.

A fellow wearing the uniform of his country's army or navy or marine corps was never under any delusions about what he could and couldn't do. Discipline is basic to military life. But many buck privates in the rear ranks or a brand-new member of a ship's crew simply walked off his base or vessel when the notion struck him. When discovered and placed under arrest—as he almost always was, sooner or later—he was listed on the roster as having been "absent without official leave."

The initial letters of the damning record, A.W.O.L., became the brand-new word *AWOL.*

AX TO GRIND

The influence of *Poor Richard's Almanac* and other publications made Benjamin Franklin one of the most widely read of early American writers.

He is a central character in one of his own stories. In the tale, a young Franklin was approached by a fellow who stopped to admire the family grindstone. In asking to be shown how it worked, the stranger offered young Ben an ax with which to demonstrate. Once his ax was sharp, the fellow walked off, laughing.

Readers should beware of people who have an *ax to grind*, for they have a hidden motive.

BACK TO SQUARE ONE

Especially during a group activity, it is common for someone to propose going *back to square one*. That is shorthand for suggesting: "Let's scrap all we have done, and start over."

Not a bad way to express the notion of giving up and making a fresh start. The expression took shape during the pre-electronic era in which board games of many kinds were in use. Several widely popular ones involved moving tokens in response to a throw of the dice or drawing of a card. At the beginning of a contest, all tokens were placed at the same starting point—square one of the board.

A proposal about going *back to square one* meant scrapping the ongoing game and starting a new one.

BACKBITE

Medieval Europe had few sports as popular as bearbaiting. An animal that was captured as a cub would be trained to fight dogs. Then the bear's owner would take him from village to village and set him against the dogs of local sporting men. These fights usually took place in some public place and constituted community outings. No admission was charged, but the bear's master would take up a collection some time during the exhibition.

Rough though the sport was, a few rules grew up to govern it. For example, the bear's master was required to fasten him to a post with a chain that could not exceed an agreed length. Owners of dogs were expected to keep their animals in hand and to let only a few attack the bear at once.

When a bear was pulled up short by reaching the end of his chain, some of the dogs would hold him at bay. Sometimes one of the pack would slip behind the bear and attack him from the rear. Unable to protect himself from such a *backbite*, the bear would let out a roar of pain and rage. Good sportsmanship outlawed backbiting, but it was a common occurrence. As early as the twelfth century the term had come to describe anyone taking an unfair advantage. Then its meaning expanded, and the expression entered modern speech to mean speaking ill of a person behind his or her back.

BACKLOG

Frontiersmen faced a serious problem when it came to starting a fire. Matches were rare, and flint and steel often failed in damp weather. Many pioneers tried to keep a fire burning without interruption for months at a time.

A big green log, next to stones in the back of a fireplace, would smolder for days. Dry wood would be laid in front of it to burn, and the next morning the back log yielded embers from which a new blaze could be started.

As a rule, the back log was not used for fuel, although it could be pulled out and burned in an emergency. Over time, any sort of reserve came to be known as a *backlog*. In contemporary parlance, a more familiar use of the term refers to an excess number of duties waiting to be performed.

BACK-SEAT DRIVER

Barney Oldfield's Ford No. 999 held only the driver. Single seats of some early cars held two or three people. Rear seats weren't added until the auto age was beyond its infancy. A back seat held additional riders, but these found it difficult to talk to the driver.

In 1912, things began to change. The four-cylinder Essex coach was offered with a boxlike body that was comfortably enclosed. Other makers soon copied the idea.

Passengers immediately took advantage of their chance to be heard. Calling for action or telling the person at the wheel where to turn or stop, any person who volunteered advice to the one in charge became known as the *back-seat driver*.

BALLYHOO

Few potentially profitable new pharmaceuticals or new models of cars come to the market without extensive *ballyhoo*. This term for attention-catching advertising sounds like it might have been coined on Madison Avenue.

Or not. Actually, advertising executives who resort to this practice may owe its name to events in faraway County Cork, Ireland. Tradition holds that residents of the village of Ballyhooly made a name for themselves by debating nearly every local issue as though the fate of the world depended upon it.

Located not far from Mallow, the town became known throughout the British Isles as a result of the way citizens talked on and on. Members of Parliament charged that some of their own debates were as loud as goings-on in Ballyhooly, and tabloid newspapers eventually adopted the comparison.

With its final syllable dropped, the name of the noisy Irish town came to label any loud debate.

BAND-AID

In one report, by the *Wall Street Journal*, experts were asked to cure a fiscal ill, and they spent a lot of time trying to make a diagnosis. Since they couldn't agree about the cause of the sickness, it was reported that "all they did was to put a Band-Aid on it."

Even the head honcho of a big pharmaceutical company didn't anticipate that its ready-made bandage would make such a hit. Little bandages in a box solved minor household problems galore but were useless in a major emergency. The popularity of Johnson & Johnson's

Band-Aid caused its name to be associated with any small adhesive bandage, and eventually with patching up a large problem as well as a small injury.

BANDWAGON

America's first great showman, Phineas T. Barnum, didn't wait for the public to come to him. Instead, he took his attractions to the people. Arriving in a city for an engagement, he would hire a high wagon of the sort used by local bands of musicians for outdoor performances.

Parading through streets with odd-looking men and women aboard wagons, "Barnum's Great Scientific and Musical Theater" was a sensation. Onlookers were encouraged to hop on the bandwagons in order to ride with the performers and add to the excitement.

Many political clubs built bandwagons of their own, then gave rolling concerts to publicize candidates. The impact of Barnum and elections on language proved lasting. Any person who agrees to become a part of a movement or campaign, or who simply joins the crowd, is described as climbing on the *bandwagon*.

BARBARIAN

Historians pay tribute to ancient Greece as the world's greatest center of culture and learning. Their judgment is not new; the Greeks themselves were proudly confident that they excelled in every area of life. Arrogance ran so high that they sneeringly referred to the speech of non-Greeks as made up of unintelligible sounds, like "bar-bar." Consequently, any foreigner came to be called *barbarus*.

Passing through Latin, the label of contempt eventually entered English as *barbarian*. Little changed by centuries of usage, the term of mockery is now applied to any rude or savage person. Its long record indicates that in every age and among all peoples, many take it for granted that anyone who speaks with an unfamiliar accent can't possibly have anything significant to say.

BARGE IN

If you barge into a conference room and take a seat, your actions will not remotely resemble those of a clumsy cargo vessel. Yet movements of such a ship gave rise to the expression.

It was brought back to Europe by Crusaders who were impressed with a small sailing vessel they saw on the Nile River. Adapting the Egyptian name, similar ships built in Britain were called *barges*.

Especially designed for use in shallow water, the barge proved useful in canals as well as in rivers. Eventually, steam replaced sails on these flat-bottom craft that were sturdy but clumsy. Accidents were frequent, for once a barge got under way it was difficult to stop it or to change course rapidly.

By 1800, shippers were comparing hasty action of any sort with the heavy rushing of a cargo boat. As a result, we continue to say that a person bursting into any situation is *barging in*.

BARK UP THE WRONG TREE

Early settlers in what is now the United States discovered a new prey for hunting. Raccoons and possums were abundant, and they could be hunted with nearly any kind of dog. When first pursued, a 'coon would run through the underbrush. But as dogs neared, the animal would climb the nearest tree. Barking and jumping underneath, dogs tried to keep their quarry at bay until hunters came to make the kill.

Sometimes, however, a shrewd animal played a trick. After climbing a tree, it worked its way through branches and across other trees to freedom—leaving dogs barking under an empty tree. This outcome of a hunting expedition was common enough to cause us to say another person is mistaken by commenting that he or she is *barking up the wrong tree*.

BARNSTORM

In the early days of traveling theater, third-rate companies didn't get the best of facilities. Many had to settle for almost any empty building. Some held one-night stands in barns.

Such a performing group didn't stay anywhere long. Entertainers stormed from place to place, sometimes having to wait for horses and cows to be removed before a stage could be improvised.

A candidate for office who raced from one spot to another, addressing small crowds, had a lot in common with a theatrical barnstormer. From amateurish performers to hack politicians, the term attached to the actions of anyone who moved around a lot without getting much done. In effect, they storm from barn to barn; hence, *barnstorm*.

BATTLE-AX

By the eleventh century, the battle-ax was a regular part of the equipment issued to British warriors. Often fastened to the wrist by means of a chain, such a weapon was indeed fearful. On June 23, 1314, the day before the famous battle of Bannockburn, Robert the Bruce felled Sir Henry Bohrn with a single blow of his battle-ax.

The invention of firearms soon made other weapons obsolete, and the battle-ax became a favorite among collectors. Specimens are prominently displayed in the Tower of London and at numerous other museums.

A first glimpse of this brutal and intimidating old weapon almost always evokes awe. As a result, comedians began to compare it with a quarrelsome and irritable person. Since performers were male, the butt of humor was invariably female. This usage, sexually biased though it is, leads many a modern male to mix jest with affection and refer to his wife as a *battle-ax*.

BAWL OUT

Should you ever *bawl out* a delivery person or sales clerk, your actions may remind someone of a really ornery creature.

Handlers vow that the domestic bull is the most persistent and belligerent animal on earth. When a big fellow is angry, he is mad at everybody and everything. In the Old West, every cowboy knew that when a bull was rounded up, he was likely to bellow for hours.

Angry noise made by animals was so common that a cattleman who berated another was compared with a bull and said to *bawl out* the other. Long a part of ranch talk, the term was popularized by writer Rex Beach. It caught the public imagination and soon swept the country as a way to describe a vigorous vocal display of anger.

BAY WINDOW

At least as early as the fourteenth century, architects devised a novel type of window. Projecting outward from the wall of the house, it is sometimes made as a rectangle and sometimes as a semicircle. Because it gives a room a recess like a tiny harbor, or bay, sailors called it a *bay window*.

Footnote: In America in the 1890s, some imaginative person transferred its name to the bulging human paunch.

BEAN POLE

Beans have been cultivated for a long, long time. Early ones served mostly to provide feed and litter for animals. So when a climbing variety turned out to bear seeds that humans liked, it became a garden favorite.

Named for the color of its flower, the scarlet runner was recognized as a real curiosity—it twined in a direction opposite to the apparent motion of the sun. In the story of "Jack and the Beanstalk," this queer vine played a central role.

Stakes or poles are essential to growing scarlet runners. Six feet or more in length, these poles are saved for reuse season after season. These special pieces of gardening gear are often compared with tall, lean persons. Abraham Lincoln thought little of it when he was called "a *bean pole* of a country lawyer."

For many years this old garden term has been used as a label for a slender person of above average height.

BEAT AROUND THE BUSH

Noblemen and gentry who went in for the sport of boar hunting were glad for others to do the dangerous work. So they employed young males who fanned out through the woods and swamps, making noise in order to beat animals toward the hunters.

The razor-sharp teeth of a big boar were lethal weapons no one wanted to encounter. Unarmed beaters frequently stayed out of dense clumps of undergrowth where a boar might be hiding. So many of them *beat around the bush* instead of going through it that their tactic came to label any evasive technique.

BEAT THE RAP

Courtroom procedures change more slowly than many other customs. One of them, the formal rapping of a gavel, has served for centuries to open and close legal sessions. In the nineteenth century, so long as testimony was being heard or deliberations were in progress, the accused had a chance. Even the pronouncement of sentence did not close the case; the situation was not hopeless until the judge rapped on his desk. Defense attorneys used every possible means to *beat the rap* or to prevent their clients from being sentenced. Consequently, the expression now stands for any method of avoiding a penalty.

BEHIND THE SCENES

Development of the theater proceeded rapidly during the long reign of England's Queen Elizabeth I. However, more attention was given to scripts and actors than to stage settings. Most performances took place before backdrops of simple curtains.

James I and Charles I encouraged free spending in the arts. Under their sponsorship, craftsmen began making elaborate painted slides and hangings for backdrops on a stage. Such pieces, which often represented landscapes, were known simply as *scenes.*

In many plays and operas, important action was not represented on stage; instead it was simply reported to the audience. This was especially the case with murders and executions, which were often treated as having taken place between acts.

Patrons joked about the fact that many events occurred, not on the stage, but *behind the scenes.* Hence real-life action hidden from the public came to be described by the term born in the theater.

BELOW THE BELT

Rules of boxing were informal and often irregular until modern times. With some assistance, the eighth Marquis of Queensberry drew up a code that was adopted in the 1860s.

It was not acceptable, said the new rules, to hit whatever vital spot could be reached. Any blow directed to an opponent's groin would be ruled a foul.

Blows that landed in the outlawed area cost some old-timers heavily, so newcomers to the ring became more cautious. Spreading into general speech, a verbal haymaker that violates accepted standards is said to have landed *below the belt.*

BESIDE THE MARK

In medieval England, every village had its green where yeomen gathered for archery practice. This was the national pastime that produced skilled bowmen for military use.

For a target, the medieval marksmen used a bit of cloth or leather attached to a tree. Arrows that missed this mark or hit the tree *beside the mark* reduced an archer's score. Villagers took their competition so seriously that the bowman's term entered general speech to designate anything irrelevant or not to be counted.

BEST FOOT FORWARD

For a period of several centuries, European noblemen and wealthy gentry were greatly concerned about beauty of person. They affected ruffled sleeves, powdered wigs, black satin knee breeches, and full-length hose above buckled shoes.

Many of the idle rich were quite vain and took pride in showing off a good pair of legs. Some went so far as to give preference to one leg as being more attractive than the other. Such a fellow wanted to make the greatest possible sensation at levees and balls. So he found a place where he could stand with his best-looking leg and foot in front, where it would attract many glances.

By the sixteenth century, a person wanting to make a good impression knew just what to do. He put his *best foot forward* and by doing so helped to create a phrase we still use.

BETTER HALF

Puritans and other zealots brought many religious terms into common speech. Doctrine said that the soul and body, together, make up a person. Since the spiritual self was considered more important, it came to be called the *better half.*

It took a genius to see new meaning in the old expression. Writing in his *Arcadia*, Sir Philip Sidney applied it to the husband-wife union rather than the body-soul bond.

Long used to indicate either partner in the half-and-half match that is marriage, the inherited term was modified by male gallantry. For some generations, every husband with a spark of love has called the woman who makes up 50 percent of his life his *better half*.

BIG SHOT

Largely self-taught, John A. B. Dahlgren designed some of the largest guns used in the Civil War. A cannon that took his name, immense at the breech and tapering toward the muzzle, played decisive roles in numerous battles.

A sailor or soldier who saw an eleven-inch Dahlgren for the first time was often speechless. This big gun made earlier ones seem tiny and powerless. Fighting men compared an admiral or a general with the huge weapon and called the man in command a *big gun*.

Since Dahlgren's big guns spewed big shot at the enemy, any person of great importance was also known as a *big shot*.

BIGOT

Your circle of acquaintances is unusual if it doesn't include at least one outspoken bigot. Racial, religious, and political intolerances continue to flourish all over the world.

A legend has it that the word *bigot* was born of a dramatic incident at the court of King Charles III of France, known as Charles the Simple. As the story goes, he demanded absolute obedience and required noblemen to kneel in order to kiss his foot.

One stout fellow, Rollo of Normandy, was led before the king for the customary ceremony. At the last minute, he decided not to conform. So instead of kneeling, the story goes, he held himself erect and blurted: "*Ne se, bi got!*" (No, by God!) Charles scolded him severely, and as a result, any person who doesn't accept conventional standards came to be known as a *bigot*.

That colorful tale may have been invented as a result of the fact that *"Bi got!"* really was a commonly used oath among Germanic peoples. It was bestowed on Norman invaders of England as a mocking nickname. Possibly this helped to form the label we apply to stubbornly opinionated people.

BIGWIG

Had not sheep been abundant in England until modern times, you might not include in your vocabulary a term from British legal practices.

Skins complete with wool were widely used in manufacture of wigs. A judge could be distinguished from ordinary folk at a glance; his enormous powdered wig identified his office. Court officials were not the only persons who donned this special regalia, but they were often seen by members of the public.

A man who could decide the fate of another was clearly a person of great importance. Consequently, anyone in a position of authority came to be called a *bigwig*.

BIKINI

In 1947, the first swimsuit designed to reveal practically every asset of a woman's figure went on sale. Wondering what to call the daring garment, makers noticed that males who saw it for the first time reacted like it was an atomic bomb.

Scientists used the Marshall Islands in 1946 for a crucial experiment. Having moved 167 natives to Rongerik, "Operation Crossroads" head William H. R. Blandy used the Bikini atoll for tests of the atomic bomb.

Comparing the impact of the new swimsuit to the world-shaking events in the Pacific, fashion experts called it the *Bikini*.

Once that name was given to the explosive garment, the only change has been the dropping of its capitalization.

BITE THE BULLET

Next time you are caught between a rock and a hard place, with no good way out, you may decide to *bite the bullet* and push ahead. Sometimes that is the only alternative to calling things quits.

That was the case with many Civil War casualties. Carried from the field with a mangled arm or leg, Billy Yank or Johnny Reb could not turn away when a surgeon with a bloody apron approached with a scalpel or saw.

With lives hanging in the balance, supplies of whiskey and other painkillers often ran out. That meant the best the medics could do for a fellow was to offer him a soft-lead bullet. Placed between the teeth, it did not give much relief, but it was better than nothing. It made amputation a little easier to bear if he could *bite the bullet* instead of lying on the table screaming.

BITTER END

Many early English ships were equipped with a bitt, or heavy log mounted on an axle. With one end of a cable attached to the bitt, the other was tied to an anchor. Should anything happen to the bitt, a ship was in trouble—for there was no way to drop anchor in order to resist winds and tides.

In some waters, even a very long cable was not adequate. Played out until no more was wrapped around the bitt, it still didn't permit the anchor to touch bottom.

Such a situation was always alarming and often dangerous. As a result, any unpleasant final result came to be called a *bitter end*.

BITTER PILL TO SWALLOW

Any unpleasant news may be called a *bitter pill to swallow*. Figuratively applied to a wide range of situations, the expression was once painfully literal.

For centuries, a physician's pellet for use in sickness has been known as a *pill*. Honey and spices were about all that doctors had with which to try to mask disagreeable components. Bark of a New World tree, the cinchona, was effective in fighting malaria. But the quinine it contains is extremely bitter. Widely employed in the era before medications were coated, cinchona pellets caused any disagreeable thing to be termed a *bitter pill to swallow*.

BLACK LIST

Deans of noted British colleges and universities often had to deal with misconduct. Many kept ledgers in which they recorded the names and misdeeds of students who broke rules. A dean's register of offenses was typically bound in black, so the records it held made up his *black list*.

Owners of business firms were less precise about notebooks used in order to jot names of customers who didn't pay promptly. A record of people who should be denied credit took the campus label, in spite of the fact that a merchant's black list might be kept in a blue or brown book.

From these specialized usages, the *black list* expanded in meaning. Today it names any kind of record that identifies persons who should be denied membership or watched carefully.

BLACK SHEEP

Efficient methods of processing wool are quite modern. As late as the 1700s, cleaning fibers shorn from sheep was a major operation, and dyeing was even more difficult. Only a few satisfactory dyestuffs were known, and those were expensive. In this situation, ordinary folk used vast quantities of undyed fleece.

Under these conditions, off-color wool was low in value. Black sheep were rare, and unless a man owned many flocks he was not likely to produce enough black fleece to market it. Except for mutton, a dark-haired animal was practically worthless to the small farmer. Generations of herdsmen berated the *black sheep* with such vigor that its name attached to any scamp or renegade.

BLACKBALL

Members of some private clubs still vote on applicants for admission. Few, however, adhere to the time-honored custom of casting anonymous ballots by means of dropping marbles or balls into a hat or box.

When little spheres constituted votes, white or pink signified "yes," while black meant "no." In many instances, a single black ball caused a candidate to be rejected.

Clubs, fraternities, and sororities are today more likely to use an electronic device than a hat or a handful of marbles. Yet it may take only one negative vote to *blackball* an applicant.

BLACKMAIL

Though *blackmail* has come to stand for illegal extortion, it originated among respectable farmers of Scotland. As late as the sixteenth century, most of their farmland was owned by English noblemen. These absentee landlords charged very high rent. From the ancient Scottish term for tribute, such rent was called *mail*. Rental agreements always stipulated that payment be made in silver or white mail.

Farmers who had no cash were sometimes permitted to pay in produce or black mail. Since prices fluctuated so much, greedy landlords often took advantage of penniless tenants and squeezed out black mail worth a great deal more than the cash amount of the rent.

People who extort hush money from a guilty party are as merciless as the landlords were in dealing with their tenants. *Blackmail* came to mean a bribe paid to one person holding an advantage over another.

BLOCKBUSTER

Any time a *blockbuster* movie or novel is released, lines are sure to form. Producers and publishers know that the glow won't last long, so they want to cash in while they can.

The earliest blockbusters stayed in the news for month after month during World War II. The original *blockbuster* was a high-explosive bomb that could level an entire block.

Eventually, anything that made a considerable impact, like a spectacularly successful enterprise or production, took the name of the most powerful bomb before the advent of nukes.

BLOCKHEAD

Until the 1300s, few English men or women except members of the nobility wore hats. Then hoods went out of fashion in the space of two or three generations, and all sorts of men began wearing hats of leather and felt. Some of the most popular styles were shaped like thimbles, while other styles resembled sugar loaves.

Hat makers multiplied and formed guilds in which expert craftsmen became adept at pleasing their customers—almost all of whom were males. They learned how to make imitation beaver from goat's wool and how to use head-shaped blocks of yew or oak in forming hats that fit snugly and held their shape.

In time such "block heads" became standard gear among hatters. By the time Henry VIII ascended the throne, dull-witted persons were being compared with dummy heads in hat shops. As a result, it became standard usage to label a dolt or simpleton a *blockhead*.

BLOG

We have an information explosion on our hands, and it's at arm's length. Anyone with a computer and access to a phone or cable connection has the potential to reach, and preach to, millions of fellow Web users.

The Internet is saturated with millions of Web sites, many created by individuals using their sites as a launching pad to editorialize on myriad topics. This phenomenon has given rise to a new generation of information dispensers, whom we refer to as *bloggers. Blogger* is a derivation of the term *blog,* short for *Weblog.* According to Webopedia.com, a *blog* is "a Web page that serves as a publicly accessible personal journal for an individual. Typically updated daily, blogs often reflect the personality of the author."

Blogs, and bloggers, achieved an unprecedented level of notoriety during the 2004 presidential campaign. Blogging blabbers on all sides of the political spectrum weighed in with their sharp analyses of the candidates. Their combined influence played as great a role in shaping public opinion as did any TV network, cable news show, or other media outlet.

BLOW OFF STEAM

It took years for trainmen to learn how to handle locomotives. Hot fires were required in order to keep up enough steam to move. But when an engine halted, steam pressure could rise quickly. There were no safety valves; at intervals, the engineer had to pull a lever and blow off the steam to prevent an explosion.

In the 1830s, a locomotive was a thing of awe when quiet and still. Anyone who for the first time saw the iron monster blow off steam never forgot the incident.

Observers compared such an explosive incident with a sudden display of temper. Soon adopted into the speech of merchants and travelers, anyone indulging in a colorful outburst was said to *blow off steam*.

BLOWOUT

Davy Crockett used to say that a fellow who turned red in the face and started hollering was having a *blowout*.

Town and city folk picked up the expression coined by tellers of tall tales and used it to mean an outburst of anger. By the time Washington Irving and Sir Walter Scott put the word into their novels, everybody knew what it meant.

But a rush of hot air from an early pneumatic tire made a blowout by a riverboat gambler seem tame. Seventy pounds of pressure against thin rubber on unpaved roads made tires almost as explosive as liquid refreshments at a big shindig.

Thicker, tougher tires and asphalt roads cut down on highway blowouts, so our living language turned back upon itself. With frontier emphases revived, you are now a lot more likely to be involved in a *blowout* in someone's living room or den than on the interstate.

BLUE JEANS

Many European cities once specialized in making a distinctive cloth of some kind. Heavy twilled cotton from Janua (modern Genoa) was called *jean* after its point of origin. In 1495, King Henry VIII of England bought 262 bolts of it. Jeans, or male garments made from jean, were prized because they didn't wear out quickly.

Undyed fabric was used for generations before a batch of cloth dyed blue was turned over to cutters and sewers. The resulting *blue jeans* quickly made undyed ones obsolete.

BLUE RIBBON

Partly because blue dye of good quality was scarce and expensive, rulers of at least two nations elevated the color to prominence.

In France, induction into the ancient order of the Holy Ghost was the highest honor a knight could achieve. Membership in it was symbolized by a blue scarf that ordinary people were forbidden to wear.

English monarchs who wished to confer lasting honor upon a soldier or civil servant bestowed the Order of the Garter, represented by a ribbon of bright blue.

Inevitably, judges of contests began awarding blue ribbons to persons who placed first. Whether or not a strand of fabric is used, anyone who wins or is awarded a *blue ribbon* knows that it signifies the highest possible honor.

BOMBSHELL

Gunpowder sheathed in metal came into use long ago, but most early bombs were small and crude. Big and sophisticated ones, designed to be shot from cannon, were used in World War I. For the first time, a powerful explosive charge could be sent into enemy ranks.

Regardless of how close it came to its target, an exploding bombshell was an object of fearful admiration. It packed a punch like nothing else.

G.I.s who lived through a hail of German shells came home with a new and descriptive label for an explosively attractive female. That's how Marilyn Monroe became famous as "the blonde *bombshell*"—though the term of admiration was also applied to numerous other celebrities.

BONANZA

As long as ships were at the mercy of winds, fair weather was highly prized. From the Latin word *bonus*, meaning "good," evolved the word *bonanza*, used by Spanish sailors to name clear days after a hard blow.

In time the sea term came to indicate good fortune in general. During the California gold rush beginning in 1848, American miners borrowed the term from the Spanish with whom they came in contact. It became a household word after one of the world's greatest gold rushes took place in the Yukon Territory of northwest Canada, beginning in 1896. Today *bonanza* applies to any source of great wealth or prosperity.

BONFIRE

There is nothing quite like the combination of festivity and food at an evening picnic that includes a bonfire.

This source of fun and frolic is particularly American, but we borrowed the word *bonfire* from our English ancestors. It once referred to a *bone-fire,* which was a primitive form of cremation. After the practice was abandoned by ordinary folk, it was observed with bodies of saints. Ashes from the burning of a saint's bones were potent good luck charms.

When roaring blazes ceased to be used to consume bones, the spelling of *bone-fire* changed, and any hearty outdoor fire came to be known as a *bonfire.*

BOOB TUBE

Before the advent of flat screens and high-definition television, all TVs functioned by means of a cathode ray tube. This factor, plus the shapes of early sets, fostered the use of the term *the tube* to designate a television set of any kind or size. Derogatory remarks about the quality of material seen on the tube prompted many Americans to begin sneering at the television, calling it the *boob tube.* Although digital television is sure to take over in the third millennium, such a tubeless set is likely to continue to be called the *boob tube.*

BOOKMARK

During the infancy of printed books, users didn't like to risk damage by turning pages unnecessarily. Instead, they used slips of leather, fabric, or paper to mark their place. The aristocracy and those in some monastic orders used extremely elaborate bookmarks that took scores of man-hours to produce.

With a single keystroke, today's computer users can insert a *bookmark* at any desired point in a word-processed document or a CD-ROM. Marked in such a fashion, a word or paragraph can be accessed almost instantly without opening a book or turning a single page.

TO BOOT

The phrase *pulled himself up by his bootstraps* is used admiringly to describe a self-made success. Drawing only on his or her own inner resources, without help from any outside source, this person has made a mark in life.

Early computer programmers faced an obstacle: the memories of their computers were wiped clean each time the machines were turned off. To address this problem, the programmers needed to enter a short program called a *bootstrap loader* each time the machine was turned on. Once this program was read, the computer could then perform more complex functions. The short program gave the machine a "bootstrap" it could then use to perform tasks; without it, the computer was useless.

Over time, programmers figured out ways to design software so computers could perform this function automatically, and bootstrap loaders are now part of the basic makeup of any operating system. Pulling oneself up by the bootstrap is a means of restarting one's situation. The expression lives on in the phrase *to boot,* which today simply means to turn on, but reflects decades of efforts of computer programmers to make computers easier to use.

BOOZE

Little or nothing is known about Philadelphia merchant E. G. Booze, says tradition, except that he is commemorated in everyday speech. According to a common story, he bought moonshine whisky anywhere he could get it. A bottle shaped like a log cabin was his standard container, but it lacked the customary maker's label.

Customers who liked his prices didn't quibble over brand names, and they applied the merchant's name to a bottle of his stuff. Since Philadelphia was a major city, its term for unlabeled whisky spread from that center into every town and village.

That story about E. G. Booze seems to have taken shape because there is no solid evidence about the origin of the word that is now universally familiar. Possibly rooted in an old Dutch term meaning "to drink to excess," it disappeared from use for generations. Revived perhaps four centuries ago, it began to be spelled as it sounds, producing our universally familiar but mystery-shrouded *booze*.

BOTTOM DOLLAR

Novels and television dramas to the contrary, metallic dollars were never abundant in this country. During the first eighty years of U.S. coinage, only eight million silver dollars were struck. Fewer than nineteen million gold pieces were ever produced.

Most wealth was in terms of raw materials rather than in the coins of the realm. Even fur traders and buffalo hunters who swarmed in and out of St. Louis had comparatively few dollars from the mint. A typical hoard might include only a dozen or so.

Such a stack of coins never reached very high, and it didn't take skill or intelligence to know when a person came to the bottom. Because the *bottom dollar* was a signal to get back to the man's traps and guns, it came to symbolize the end of one's resources.

BOYCOTT

Have you ever participated in a *boycott* in which you refuse to buy certain merchandise? Persons who engage in protests of this sort are following the example of Irish farmers.

During the era of the famous potato famine, Captain Charles C. Boycott was managing the estates of the Earl of Erne. When tenants couldn't pay, they were evicted.

Bands of County Mayo citizens got together and launched organized resistance. Merchants refused to sell to Boycott. He was hung in effigy and greeted with jeers when he appeared in public. Many of his employer's fences were torn down. Household servants were subjected to such harassment that they slipped away and sought other jobs.

This protest movement was so successful that Captain Boycott eventually left Ireland. Attached to organized protest movements, his name lingered in speech. By the time he had been gone twenty-five or thirty years, the Irish Land League launched *boycotts* against persons who didn't agree to its demands.

Such an imprint was made that the overseer's name has entered half a dozen languages to label refusal to deal with a business, an employer, a nation, or a line of merchandise.

BRAINSTORM

Anytime you come up with a really new idea, it may be the product of individual or group brainstorming.

F. W. H. Myers, a distinguished leader of investigators, founded the Society of Psychical Research in 1882. His movement soon became the talk of the Western world. With initial study coming to focus upon telepathy, editors compared it with radio and suggested that brain waves make it possible. Engineers already knew that electrical storms affect many types of communication. That made it an easy step to compare a radio that acted strangely with an electrical storm in the brain.

Still far from understanding such states, we know that they somehow foster creativity and spontaneity. This explains why *brainstorming* is regularly sponsored by some of our biggest research laboratories and corporations.

BRASS TACKS

Just why getting down to *brass tacks* should mean abandoning the preliminaries and getting down to business, no one knows positively. The only plausible explanation traces the expression to early dry-goods stores.

Piece goods were sold by the yard, and merchants found it convenient to put tacks in the edge of the counter to indicate a yard, half-yard, and quarter-yard. Only brass-headed tacks resisted rust and remained clearly visible.

Since the practice of putting price tags on merchandise had not been introduced, the frugal purchaser inquired the price of an article. If the price was considered too high, a period of haggling was likely to follow. Once that came to an end, the merchant might say, "All right; now let's get down to *brass tacks* and mea-sure the cloth."

Intense and prolonged dickering made no sales. Only when cloth went down on the counter alongside the brass-headed tacks that measured it was any business actually transacted.

BREAK THE ICE

London, Leningrad, and many other great cities grew strong and important as a result of being situated on rivers and channels. This geographical advantage was worth little, however, in periods of bitter cold. Even large ships could become icebound, making them useless for weeks.

Small, sturdy ships known as *icebreakers* were developed to precede traveling ships and make a way through the ice. Such work was preliminary to the central task of transporting goods through freezing water.

Every veteran boatman knew that he often had to *break the ice* before actually getting down to business. Consequently, the water-born expression came to label any method of making a start.

BRING HOME THE BACON

This expression for success in competition came into vogue from a prize given for happy marriages. At the church of Dunmow, in Essex County, England, a flitch of bacon was given annually to the man and woman who, after a year of matrimony, were judged to have lived in greatest harmony and fidelity. The earliest recorded case of the awarding of the bacon took place in 1445.

By the end of the sixteenth century, couples that came forward to seek the prize were questioned before a jury of six bachelors and six maidens. Only those who gave satisfactory proof of domestic felicity gained the coveted pork. It was awarded at irregular intervals until late in the nineteenth century.

Since the phrase was widely publicized in literature, the fact that successful claimants actually did *bring home the bacon* from Dunmow led to the application of the phrase to victory in general.

BRONX CHEER

Babies discover very early that the range of sounds they can produce is almost infinite. A perennial favorite is made by placing the tongue between the lips and blowing vigorously. Ensuing vibrations, commonly known as *raspberries*, produce sounds familiar to nearly every parent.

Large numbers of adults didn't often make that sound simultaneously in the relatively sedate era that ended with World War I. But in

Yankee Stadium, fans sitting shoulder-to-shoulder were anything but sedate in the 1920s.

Few games passed without a bad call by an official or an awkward play by one of Babe Ruth's teammates. Anything that drew the ire of the masses came to evoke a chorus of raspberries. This unique chorus of sounds was heard so often in the Bronx stadium that the vibrating noise enjoyed by infants came to be known everywhere as a *Bronx cheer*.

BROWSER

Turned loose in a lush grass-covered field, nearly every horse, cow, or other domestic animal will move from one especially tender clump of grass to another, browsing through the field. The term *browser* came to be applied to a shopper flitting from one spot in a store to another or to a reader flipping from page to page in a book.

Today's most frequent *browser* is neither an animal nor a person. Instead, it is computer software designed for incredibly fast "picking and choosing" from many spots on the World Wide Web. This high-tech *browser* offers a choice of sites that promises— maybe—to have the clump of information for which the user is searching.

BUCCANEER

Americans who fondly remember swashbuckling movies will be surprised to learn that the word *buccaneer* equates with "barbecuer."

The English borrowed the French word *boucanier*, which referred to a person on the Caribbean island of Hispaniola or Tortuga who hunted wild oxen or boars and then cooked them over a fire on a frame called a *boucan*.

Soon English, French, and Dutch *boucaniers* had a remunerative business intercepting Spanish galleons laden with gold that were plowing the seas home to Spain from the South American mines. The first recorded use in English of *buccaneer* in this sense was in 1690.

One of the most famous buccaneers was Henry Morgan, who was even knighted by the king of England for capturing and destroying the city of Panama, which belonged to England's enemy, Spain. However, by 1700 these buccaneers began attacking ships of all nations, and the British, French, and Dutch governments classified them as pirates who were outlaws.

A modern *buccaneer* is a ruthless speculator or adventurer in business or politics.

BULLDOZER

In the aftermath of the Civil War, many Louisiana vigilantes called themselves *bulldozers*. This was because overseers had traditionally exacted upon slaves punishment that was likened to doses of punishment fit for a bull. Postwar bulldozers carried a black-snake whip and at least one big pistol. When such a fellow moved into action, people got out of his way in a hurry. Long dormant, the terrorist name was revived prior to World War II. It seemed an appropriate word to designate a powerful earth-moving machine that easily pushed opposition aside.

After being widely used in military operations, the mechanical *bulldozer* became standard equipment in construction work.

BULLPEN

Large numbers of civilians were placed under military arrest during the Civil War. Prisons were not large enough to accommodate everyone charged, perhaps, with "giving a hurrah for Jeff Davis."

To hold large numbers of prisoners, temporary stockades were built. Because such a structure resembled a cattle pen and because persons in it were as helpless as steers, it was called a *bull pen*.

Then the wartime place of detention gave its name to an area adjoining a playing field. While warming up, relief pitchers in the *bullpen* are almost but not quite as confined as steers waiting to be loaded on a train.

BULL'S-EYE

Until it was outlawed in 1835, bull baiting was a major national sport in England. Some put their money on the dogs, others preferred the bull. Just as present-day racing enthusiasts often put their money on a *horse's nose*, British sports were prone to put a crown on the *bull's eye*.

Since the coin equivalent to five shillings was roughly the size of an eye on which it was wagered, it took the same name. Targets developed for marksmen came to include a central black spot about the size of a coin. Using the sportsman's label to designate the coin-sized spot, the center of any target became its *bull's-eye*.

BUMPED OFF

During races on the Thames and other rivers of England, boats were launched one at a time. When a crew caught up with a rival and bumped its shell, the latter was disqualified. Popular meets meant heavy gambling, so many a spectator groaned or cheered when a boat was bumped out of the race.

London's underworld borrowed from the sporting world and began to say that a person coming to a violent end had been *bumped off*. Famous mystery writer Edgar Wallace picked up the expression and used it in some of his thrillers.

During the Prohibition era, gangsters *bumped off* so many rivals that the boating term from England became fixed in American speech.

BURY THE HATCHET

Trappers and soldiers in contact with American Indians on the frontier knew little about native customs. In addition, most of them didn't care to learn.

White men mistakenly believed that the stone tomahawk had no use except in battle. Among some tribes, ceremonial burial of a weapon signaled that a period of war had come to an end.

Perhaps jokingly, it came to be said that when conflict ended, a warrior would cover his weapon with earth so he wouldn't be tempted to use it on the skull of a foe.

No tomahawk was remotely like a metal hatchet of the white man, and Indian weapons were given ceremonial interment only among a few cultures. Yet when an opponent ceases to fight or a spouse stops battling with words, he or she is still said to *bury the hatchet*.

BUSH LEAGUE

Any sparsely settled area aside from a desert is likely to abound in bushes and trees. Not simply in modern times, but for many centuries, urban dwellers have been prone to look down their noses at bush country.

Small cities located in such regions cannot pay the freight in order to have major league baseball teams. A minor confederation is the best that such a place can afford.

Spreading from baseball talk, even if located in the heart of Manhattan, a small enterprise is likely to be disparaged as *bush league*.

BUSHED

When you find yourself exhausted at the end of an unusually hard day, you may describe yourself as being *bushed*. If so, you can thank the early Dutch settlers in the New World for the colorful word.

Some of them came from the crowded Low Countries early in the seventeenth century. For a generation, thousands left their homeland every year. Wilderness land and uncleared forest tracts were called *bosch* by these Dutch settlers. English-speaking neighbors modified their word and began describing any dense region as *bush country*.

Even the hardiest of adventurers sometimes found bush so thick that it seemed to get the better of him. After a particularly difficult time trying to hack out a trail, a fellow was likely to protest that he was *bushed*, or exhausted. Spreading from the frontier, the American-born term is now included in the vocabulary of ordinary folk as well as outdoorsmen and adventurers.

BUTTONHOLE

In the early nineteenth century, men's coats could be buttoned all the way up to the neck. Except in extreme weather, however, it was customary to leave the coat open at the throat. The unused buttons proved a great advantage to gossips and businessmen alike. A man with a yarn to spin or goods to sell would stop to talk with a victim. In order to prevent a hurried escape, the talker would seize a button and hold it. Thus the term *buttonhold* came into existence.

When fashion decreed a change in the design of men's coats, both of the upper-front edges were folded back to form lapels, and the upper buttons were eliminated.

No longer having a top button to grasp, an eager talker often took hold of his victim's lapel. Since *buttonhold* sounds so much like *buttonhole,* by 1860 *buttonhole* was being used to name the act of forcing attention upon a reluctant listener.

BYTE

When computers were rare and very expensive, users of binary notation modified and combined *binary* and *digit* to form the name for a cluster of eight adjoining bits designating a letter or numeral, such as *G* or *9*. Though wholly artificial, *byte* has entered scores of languages and is one of the few words that is likely to have the same meaning regardless of where it is encountered.

CAMEO ROLE

Seashells and gemstones often have several layers that include two or more hues. Long ago, artisans learned to take advantage of this factor by carving in such fashion that a raised central figure is of different color from the background.

A cameo engraved in this way doesn't have to be rare and costly in order to be beautiful and prized. Many that are hawked on the streets of Rome and other European cities are inexpensively exquisite, though tiny.

Transferred to the world of entertainment, the name of small but lovely jewelry became the term for a bit part played by a notable performer. On the stage, in the movies, and in television, many producers vie for viewers by including *cameo roles* that feature persons with famous names.

CAPRICIOUS

When you are forced regularly to spend time with a *capricious* person, you tend to find your companion quite annoying. Anyone who frequently indulges in impulsive changes of mind is hard to deal with. Italians of past generations wouldn't have challenged that verdict. Matter of fact, they coined the descriptive term as a result of watching goats in action.

No other domestic animal quite matches the goat in its tendency to switch suddenly from frolicking to butting heads. Many a goatherd noticed that animals seemingly intent upon grazing could be mating in the blink of an eye.

Called the *caper* by Romans, the animal's behavior led humans to label outlandish conduct as cutting capers. Italians who knew the goat as the *capriccio* adapted its name to describe a person subject to erratic whims and sudden willful behavior.

CARRY A TORCH

Torchlight parades were common features of political campaigns in rural America. Accompanied by drums or other musical instruments, an evening demonstration was likely to be loud and colorful.

Only enthusiastic followers took part in such rallies. A fellow who carried a torch didn't care who knew that he was wholeheartedly behind his candidate.

It was an easy transition to move from describing a passionate political follower to speaking of an ardent lover. These days, many a man or woman will *carry a torch* for someone not interested in winning a political office.

CARVED IN STONE

If you cite a long-prevalent social standard as a guide for present-day conduct, someone is likely to protest that it isn't *carved in stone*. Alive and well today, this saying is rooted in antiquity.

One of Scripture's most dramatic stories describes the encounter in which Moses received the Ten Commandments. Artists typically depict the bearded prophet descending from a mountain carrying these important rules of conduct. They are carved into stone, so that no word—not even a single letter—can be altered.

Standards of behavior or inherited ways, compared with the laws received by Moses, may be dismissed as not *carved in stone*. That is, they are far from timeless and are subject to change.

CATBIRD SEAT

Anytime you are in complete control of a situation, you are sitting in the *catbird seat*.

That often was the case with persons who tried their luck at pioneer sportscaster Red Barber's poker table. When he was sure that there was an ace in the hole, he whispered that he was sitting in the catbird seat.

Red's memory of tales heard in youth may have influenced him. Tall tales transmitted orally in the Southeast praise the catbird as being the smartest of all wild, feathered creatures.

Intrigued by his poker-playing friend's vivid expression, James Thurber called one of his famous stories "The Catbird Seat." Introduced into everyday speech by Thurber, the phrase has proved so resilient that no one describes a position of advantage as a bluebird's seat or a redbird's seat.

CAUGHT RED-HANDED

A common felony of the past involved the butchering of another person's pig, sheep, or cow. Under legal codes that prevailed for generations, possession of freshly killed meat did not constitute proof of guilt. Only a man caught with the blood of an animal on his hands was sure to be convicted.

It was a waste of breath to plead for mercy after having been *caught red-handed*. That happened frequently enough for the expression naming guilt to survive long after most folk ceased to raise their own meat. Now we use it to indicate detection of an act of stealth—whether or not a law is violated.

CHAPERONE

French priests and others in the early Middle Ages wore a special type of hood, which they called a *chaperon*, meaning "little mantle." This hood crossed the English Channel with the Norman Conquest and was for many years worn only by men. Edward III made the chaperon part of the full-dress costume worn by members of the Order of the Garter when he founded it in 1349.

In the same spirit that led modern women to adopt slacks, medieval ladies began to wear their lords' chaperon. For more than a century, the garment was fashionable. Then it fell into disuse, and only old ladies who cared nothing about fashion continued to wear it. They were the sort often designated to watch over young girls. As late as 1830, it was said that any attractive miss was likely to be guarded by an old biddy wearing a chaperon.

Eventually the garment disappeared, but its name stuck to guardians of conduct with the result that the *chaperone* was a fixture of American life until recent times.

CHARLEY HORSE

Many gym attendants or trainers of athletes can tell you all about *charley horses.*

The story is that at the old Chicago White Sox ballpark, there was an old horse named Charley. All during the 1890s, he was used to pull a roller across the infield. His work was repetitive, so his leg muscles got so stiff he could hardly walk. Players and spectators who suddenly caught a cramp thought of the old fellow and called it a *charley horse.*

Though that explanation doesn't hold up under scrutiny, it survives because there is no solid alternative. Before veterinary science was widely known, jockeys and trainers used *horse ail* to name any obscure ailment of a racer. In the same era, a night watchman was a *charlie*—whose pounding of the cobblestones probably produced many an aching muscle. Foot or leg cramps experienced by a charlie could have been compared with ailments of a lame animal in order to produce the term *charley horse.*

CHECKMATE

Few expressions have a more ancient lineage than *checkmate*. Now synonymous with "to thwart" or "to frustrate," it was long restricted to the game of chess.

No one knows where chess originated or when. It was already old when early Arabs borrowed it from the Persians. Through Spanish traders, it reached Europe in the eighth century. In taking up the new game, the West adopted some of the ancient terms connected with it.

One such word was *shah* (king), designating the most important of the playing pieces. According to rules of the game, when one's shah was trapped, defeat was inevitable. An Arab who maneuvered his opponent into a hopeless position would cry, *Shah mat!* (The king is dead!) Passing through Spanish and French, this expression entered English as *checkmate* and came to name any stroke of victory.

CHEESECAKE

Measured by standards of their eras, some entertainers have been scantily clad since an early promoter first charged a fee to watch them. Until this century, however, deliberately uncovered flesh was seldom seen except in special places.

Photography and mass-circulation publications made near-nudity common, but not commonplace. Until recent decades, practically all subjects for this specialized form of art were female.

Especially in the case of a natural blonde or redhead, skin color is often remarkably close to that of a delicacy whose basic ingredient is cream cheese. It was natural—and inevitable—to compare flesh tones with food. That's why we use *cheesecake* to label big areas of bare skin and photos or performances featuring them.

CHEW THE FAT

Salt pork was basic to the diet of seamen in the great age of sailing. As none was wasted, pieces of skin were saved for emergencies. When supplies ran low, each member of the crew might receive a chunk of skin in lieu of a slice of meat.

A rind, or skin, was tough and unpalatable. But the layer of fat attached to it was better than nothing. Sailors to whom rinds were doled out chewed off the fat, then often held the skins between their teeth for an hour or two.

Casual talk was a natural accompaniment of chewing on rinds. Shipboard sessions with rancid pork were so common that the sailors' expression was adopted by landlubbers to label indulgence in idle talk.

CHICKEN FEED

Pioneers who pushed into the American West took their domestic creatures with them. Chickens were high on the list of favorites, for flocks could be brought through the winter on grain too poor for use in the kitchen.

Except for table scraps, inferior wheat and corn constituted the most common chicken feed. City slickers picked up the farm-born expression and applied it to copper and silver coins.

By the time riverboat gamblers became common, the label was being used to designate any small amount of money. One flashily dressed fellow who cleaned out a greenhorn complained that he had played all night for *chicken feed*—only twenty-three dollars.

CHIME IN

Starting some time before the fourteenth century, a way to ring the bells or chimes in a church tower was to play a simple melody by striking a bell and having the other bells echo it.

Conversations sometimes resembled the music from a cathedral tower. A person of importance would give his opinion, and others in the group would mumble agreement. Thus a person who merely echoed another's opinion was said to *chime in*.

CHIP

For centuries, a piece of wood, stone, or metal that has been broken or cut off of a larger mass has been called a *chip*. This old name became used to refer to thinly sliced wafers of potatoes, or potato chips. Other chips became popular around poker tables, roulette wheels, and many other games of chance.

In recent decades silicon, the base material of ordinary sand, was found to be a suitable material for making small wafers of semiconductor material. Once it became possible to manufacture this new kind of *chip* in quantity at low cost, the computer industry in California's Silicon Valley became a major site of its manufacture.

CHIP ON ONE'S SHOULDER

A widespread tale insists it was once common for a rural bully to threaten, "Knock this *chip off my shoulder*, if you dare!"

Even exaggerated tales do not report the use of wood chips in this fashion. Popular speech isn't restricted to reality, however. In making fun of hotheads, it was said that some didn't know dried buffalo dung when they saw it.

This special kind of earthy chip was once abundant. Imagination said a tenderfoot was likely to place it on his shoulder—constituting a challenge likely to evoke laughter instead of fear. Any fellow who walked around with a buffalo *chip on his shoulder* was constantly belligerent but not worth fighting.

CHIPS ARE DOWN

Every confrontation sooner or later gets to a point at which the *chips are down*. Everything to be said has been said; everything that can be done has been done.

At a poker table, when the final bets of a hand have been made, all the chips are down on the table. No more can be added, and none may be picked up until a winner is declared.

Finality at the table leads us to use the expression when an inescapable moment of decision is at hand.

CHOW

Your appetite may not be big enough to make you a *chow* hound, but you probably join the rest of us in enjoying putting your feet under the table.

In many parts of the Far East you can't do that, of course. But chow has been available in China for centuries. Mandarins used more elegant words, while peasants employed *chow* to name any everyday dish—including dog meat.

Early explorers and adventurers had to eat chow, often with no idea of its ingredients, in order to survive. They heard the word so often that they took it back to Europe as a label for food in general.

Chow-chow, also pure Chinese, seems to have been in use earlier than its abbreviation. When a servant performed a kowtow and said "Chow-chow!" that meant food prepared from a variety of ingredients was being offered. Since the delicacy was made from finely chopped ingredients, any chopped mixture on an American table may be offered as *chow*.

CINCH

City-bred adventurers who flocked to the California gold fields in 1849 encountered many odd customs, one of which was a novel saddle girth. Instead of using English-style bellybands with straps and buckles, Indians and Mexicans of the Southwest employed twisted horsehair ropes running between two rings.

Such a piece of gear, which the Spanish called *cincha*, was more adjustable than any equipment familiar in the East. A rider who knew how to fasten a cinch could lace a saddle so it would stay in position all day. Clumsy buckles had to be adjusted at frequent intervals. The holding power of the cinch was so great that its name entered common speech to stand for any sure thing.

CLEAN AS A WHISTLE

Should you ever be a member of a team that has to investigate finances or the conduct of an official, here's hoping you will be able to report: *"Clean as a whistle!"*

As every old-timer can tell you, a good whistle made from a reed or a piece of wood emits a clear tone—but is easily damaged. Even small particles of debris, or a few drops of moisture, will change the sound of a handmade instrument. In order to emit the pure notes intended by its maker, a whistle has to be absolutely clean. Anything or anyone as clean as a brand-new whistle or as clear as its sound is bound to be good.

All of which means that an organization or person described as *clean as a whistle* has been judged to be guiltless or flawless.

CLOUD NINE

Before the advent of adding machines and calculators, even simple arithmetic was difficult. Persons forced to wrestle with multiplication and division developed special admiration for nine, believed to be the most powerful single-digit number.

This view may have been a by-product of reverence for the Holy Trinity, since nine is three times three. As late as the Victorian Age, a person sporting the finest possible outfit was often described as being "dressed to the nines." Tradition having asserted that clouds exist in a series of successively higher layers, it was logical to label the ultimate height as *cloud nine.*

A victorious contestant or a person suddenly made exuberant seems literally to be soaring in the clouds. Naturally, therefore, someone who hits the ultimate in joy is still likely to say, "I'm on *cloud nine!*"

COASTING ALONG

Captains of ocean-going vessels, facing weeks on the water, were early advocates of speed. A windjammer headed across the Atlantic was likely to have all sails spread when the wind was strong.

By contrast with fast ships of this sort, schooners that were involved in the coastal trade seemed to be slow, even leisurely. They traveled short distances, so their masters seldom bothered to use every possible yard of canvas.

Some vessels in coastal waters may have been more hurried than they seemed. Whether that was the case or not, their apparently casual movement became proverbial. As a result, a person far from water who shows no signs of effort or haste is still described as *coasting along.*

COLD FEET

In rural Europe, a person with little money—hence unwilling to move toward a purchase—was often described as having *cold feet.* A gambler wanting out of a game could let it be known that he was dead broke by saying that his feet were cold.

With its fiscal roots forgotten, the ancient expression remains alive and well. Regardless of whether engaged in pursuit of a sweetheart or planning to change jobs, a person who suddenly withdraws from the action is labeled as having *cold feet.*

COLD-BLOODED

Long before the rise of scientific medicine, everyday experience showed that there were strong links between emotions and blood. During anger or after activity, sensations in the face and neck hint that the vital fluid has become warmer. Feelings that accompany acute fear can be interpreted to mean that blood temperature has suddenly dropped.

Medieval scholars found it striking that temperaments vary widely. Some persons easily became enraged—so furious that their blood seems to be at the boiling point. Others seldom lose their tranquility and so may be derided as passionless or *cold-blooded*.

Modern science has exploded the myth of wide variations in blood temperature among humans. But influence of the past and the association of cold-blooded reptiles with evil made a lasting impression upon speech.

Practically everyone now knows that a thermometer would show a healthy person's blood to be at 98.6 degrees or thereabouts. In spite of that, we still describe anyone considered cruel or vindictive as being *cold-blooded*.

COME TO A HEAD

Half a century before Columbus's first voyage, English farmers began cultivating an odd plant. So long as it remained young, with loosely packed leaves, it was called *colewort*—a name preserved in coleslaw. When it formed a hard loaf in July or August, the mature vegetable was known as *cabbage*.

Even in this period, many townsfolk preferred to buy vegetables rather than grow them. In dry years, they became impatient when cabbages did not come on the market as usual.

Explanations by growers centered on the fact that purchasers would simply have to be patient and wait until the plants *came to a head*. Maturing of any plan or enterprise was compared with cabbage, and the concept of *coming to a head* passed from the vegetable garden into general use.

COMMENCEMENT

It seems strange that *commencement* refers to the ceremony at which academic degrees or diplomas are conferred. "Finishment" would seem to be more logical. Yet the word was appropriate earlier, as medieval universities required their graduates to spend a period teaching beginners. *Commencement*, therefore, did not mean that a man was released from an institution but that he ceased to be a pupil and commenced to teach.

CON MAN

Hard times following the Civil War forced criminals to resort to all sorts of tricks to gain relatively small amounts of money. One of the most common was the sale of fraudulent mining stock. Investors were reluctant to advance funds without examining property, so swindlers adopted the practice of asking a victim to make a small deposit "just as a gesture of confidence." The full amount was to be paid only after a trip to the West on the part of the purchaser.

A swindler would take the money advanced and decamp. This type of trick became known as the "confidence game" because it worked only if the victim had confidence in the proposal. Anyone who practiced confidence games came to be called a *con man*. This title was applied to many types of swindlers and is still used to designate a shrewd thief who finds suckers.

CONDOM

Until the rise of AIDS prompted a surgeon-general of the United States to talk bluntly, polite conversation seldom acknowledged existence of the *condom*. Originally fashioned from lamb skins, it was around a long time before anyone spoke of it except in whispers.

A trio of famous—or infamous—English members of the fox hunting set may have been first to break the silence barrier. In 1667, Lords Rochester, Roscommon, and Dorset put their names upon a pamphlet that lauded the virtues of the device then called a *condum*. Along with many others, they credited its invention to Colonel Condum of the Royal Guards.

Condum lived in the swashbuckling era of Charles II and may have been first to discover what kinds of oil will make dried intestines soft and pliable. Another candidate for the honor of having perfected the sheath is eighteenth-century English physician Charles Condom.

Regardless of which man deserves lasting tribute for inventive genius, the name of Condum—or of Condom—became permanently attached to the now-lauded gadget rarely mentioned in public until modern times.

COOK ONE'S GOOSE

A familiar old story centers on a marvelous goose that laid a golden egg every day. Greedy owners killed the bird for the sake of eggs still in the pouch of the goose. For downright stupidity, few actions rank with the notion of killing the goose that laid the golden egg. That fable may have led some persons hoping to defeat another to threaten to *cook his goose*.

A more commonplace explanation makes more sense, however. For centuries, geese rather than chickens dominated the barnyard and were prized at Christmas and other times of feasting. When a householder was down to a single bird, he would be out of luck when that one was gone. A rival threatening total defeat might express his intentions by saying: "Old fellow, you've had it—I'm going to *cook your goose!*"

CRACKPOT

Clay pots were the most common household utensils for centuries. Since many were about the size and shape of the users' heads, the human skull was widely known as a *pot*.

Though it might be thick and strong, crude earthenware was likely to crack when dropped. Housewives compared damaged vessels with heads of peculiar or eccentric neighbors. That made it natural to speak of an odd person as wearing a cracked pot on top of his shoulders. Language then took another short step, and anyone off the norm came to be known as a *crackpot*.

CRISSCROSS

In the sixteenth and seventeenth centuries, the hornbook was the major educational tool for very young children. Actually, it wasn't a book; it was a sheet of paper fastened to a board with a handle and covered with thin, translucent horn to protect it.

Printed on the paper were the alphabet (in large and small letters), the Benediction, the Lord's Prayer, and the Roman numerals. A cross was placed at the beginning of the sheet as a tribute to the Savior.

Little scholars tried to copy this *Christ cross* or *Christ's cross* as well as the letters that followed it. Just as the pronunciation of *Christ's mass* became *Christmas,* so this became *crisscross.* By the late 1700s, any pattern of crossed lines had come to be called a *crisscross*.

CROCODILE TEARS

Greek and Roman explorers who first encountered the awesome crocodile came home with a bundle of tall tales. According to them, the creature with a huge mouthful of teeth moaned like a woman in distress in order to lure victims within snapping distance.

Once a person went down the crocodile's throat, the animal sobbed out of pity for its most recent meal. At least, that was the story circulated centuries ago and used by writers as late as the time of Shakespeare.

The tall tale was repeated orally for generation after generation. As a result, stories about *crocodile tears* caused any bogus show of contrition to take that name.

CURRICULUM

When not engaged in war, Roman troops amused themselves with games and sports. Among the favorite contests was racing a chariot, or *currus*. Early speedsters eventually modified this two-wheel racer and devised a light vehicle they called *curriculum* (little chariot). It was used so extensively that its name attached to the track, or course, on which it was driven.

With the fall of Rome, the sporting term disappeared and remained dormant until the Renaissance and the revival of interest in classical times. Learned men in Scottish universities borrowed the old racetrack word and used it to stand for the round of training along which they drove their students. Popularized by this usage, *curriculum* entered common speech in the seventeenth century as the designation for the courses of study in an educational institution.

CURSOR

A Latin term for "flowing" or "running" gave rise to the word *cursive* to describe handwriting produced in flowing style. The flow of letters that is produced when a pen is guided by skilled fingers is an impressive art. The name for this efficient and effortless writing style, in this computer age, soon was adapted and bestowed upon the small marker that moves quickly and gracefully across a computer screen. The *cursor* blinks until stimulated into action.

CUT AND DRIED

Herbal medicine, now undergoing a revival, was almost universally practiced until modern times. Shops stocked camomile, senna, and a variety of other native or imported leaves.

Practitioners wanted their medications to be compounded with precision. So it was commonplace for an herb doctor to ask for leaves that had been cut and dried, rather than those just plucked.

Soon anything ready-made was compared with leaves that had been stored in jars. Jonathan Swift applied this concept to hackneyed literary styles, and ideas or plans lacking freshness and potential for change were challenged as being *cut and dried*.

DARK HORSE

From the beginning of the democratic experiment, election of public officials has been seen as being a lot like a horse race. No one knows who will win until the votes are counted, but almost everyone has a favorite. So no disparagement is intended when a public figure compares a candidate with a spirited horse.

Legend has it that Sam Flynn of Tennessee picked up an easy living by racing a coal-black stallion named Dusky Pete. Flynn usually rode Pete into a strange town as though he were an ordinary saddle horse. Not knowing they faced a champion, local men cheerfully set up races—and lost. As a result, Flynn's *dark horse* became more than regionally noted.

Formation of a new political term was probably helped by the fact that anything dark is foreboding and unlikely. At any rate, lingo of the track entered smoke-filled convention halls. As a result, professionals often joke that an unknown who shows a chance of winning is a *dark horse* in the campaign.

DEAD AS A DOORNAIL

Anything from a withered house plant to a failed project that is beyond resurrection is likely to be described as being *dead as a doornail.*

Both mechanical and electric doorbells are of recent invention. In earlier centuries, a visitor's arrival was announced by pounding with a knocker upon a metal plate nailed to the door.

Sometimes it took several heavy blows to attract attention. That meant nails holding the knocking plate suffered a lot of punishment. Repeatedly hit on its head, such a nail had the life pounded out of it so effectively that nothing could be deader.

DEADLOCK

Wrestling was a highly developed sport at least five thousand years ago. Sculptures from temple tombs near the Nile indicate that ancient grapplers used many of the holds still in vogue.

No one knows precisely when the sport became prominent in Britain. But by the time noblemen became engrossed with chivalry, many commoners were wrestling fans.

It was not unusual for a burly yeoman to make a special move. By means of it, he could hold an opponent indefinitely but was unable to force submission. Because it killed action, a hold of this sort was called a *deadlock.* Spreading from the ring, it came to label a stalemate of any kind.

DICKER

With taxes being what they are, more and more people are engaging in unreported barter. In order to prosper in this activity, a person has to be able to *dicker*, which is to engage in the give and take needed to move a negotiation toward a mutually acceptable result.

Merchants of imperial Rome were the first to spread this term throughout Europe. Well supplied with cheap trade goods, many an entrepreneur sent an expedition into the region of barbarians where trinkets were swapped for native produce, of which furs were the most valuable.

Traders found it inconvenient to try to secure individual pelts, so they adopted a practice of buying them only in lots of ten. In Latin, *decuria* means "a set of ten," and the European natives transformed it into *dicker*. This shows that furs have affected life and speech in ways no one would suspect without looking beneath the surface of everyday words.

DIDDLY-SQUAT

Sometimes a person has no opinion or feeling about an issue. Asked to take a pro or con stance, Andy Griffith might well respond: "I don't care *diddly-squat;* it makes no difference to me."

Carnival workers who traveled from town to town working one county fair after another developed their own private language. They had to do so in order to attract potential gamblers who would pay for a chance at a gimcrack prize. *Diddle-e-squat* seems to have entered carnival talk to name money—often a nickel or a dime, since that was the going rate for a game of chance.

Frequently used to hide talk about a small amount of money, it was an easy and natural transition of the carnival term to indicate very little of anything. Only slightly modified, the expression may have entered general speech because it is just suggestive enough to seem bold and maybe vulgar.

DIVE (*noun*)

Many a nightclub and dance hall is so cheap and shoddy that there's only one thing to call it: a *dive*. We owe the birth of this title to ever-changing fads in the world of furniture.

Late in the nineteenth century, Londoners became enamored with divans—or lounges—that were modeled after Turkish originals. Any owner of a public place who could afford such opulence was proud to say that it was equipped with them.

Many smoking and gambling haunts have become financial losers. Managers let these places become rundown and disreputable, but the once-fashionable divans often remained in them. Worn and soiled furniture in the Turkish mode caused any place that included it to become more or less notorious as a *dive*.

This usage might have dropped from speech had it not been strengthened by the fact that a drinking den—legal or illegal—was often situated below ground level. This arrangement required a patron to "dive into the bar," swiftly disappearing from the sight of passersby.

DOILY

In the eighteenth century, a merchant named Doiley kept a linen shop in the Strand in London. Many rich and fashionable women were among his customers. For them he introduced a number of new fabrics, one of them being a thin type of woolen, light enough for summer wear. It was popular, for it was both "cheap and genteel." Known as *doily*, the fabric became a favorite throughout England.

Later, the elite of the nation began using a revolutionary device—the table napkin—and often cut doily into small pieces for such use. Besides being a term for a table napkin, *doily* is also a term for an ornamental mat.

DON JUAN

Your high school graduation class is unusual if it doesn't include at least one *Don Juan*. Surveys suggest that one young male in eight seeks renown as a lover—and gains it almost half the time.

Tall or short, dark or fair, the typical American loverboy can't be compared with Don Juan Ternorio. This legendary Spanish nobleman, said to have flourished in the fourteenth century, caught the attention of Mozart, among others.

No one knows where the composer got his data, but notes made for his *Don Giovanni* say that the man whose name was given to the opera had 2,594 mistresses. He didn't make it to 2,595 because he was lured to a monastery. Monks who were furious that he gave the region such a bad reputation reputedly killed him—not in bed, but fully clothed and even wearing his boots.

DONNYBROOK

When a fracas erupts in a crowded place, it's hard to be an innocent bystander. Such a spontaneous melee deserves a mysterious name, but why *donnybrook*?

Because the town of Donnybrook in County Dublin, Ireland, was for generations the scene of a yearly bash. In connection with a fair held there, revelers made it a custom to drink and celebrate so boisterously that authorities came to expect a rash of fistfights on the closing night.

About 1855, Donnybrook abolished the fair and put an end to annual brawls. But *donnybrook* was already in general use as a name for anything from a loud argument to a riot.

DOUBLE TAKE

Have you ever been stopped short by a subliminal glimpse of something and didn't believe what you saw? That common experience calls for a second and closer look—a *double take*.

Whether working on a set or in a studio, many a director has called for the camera to take another look at a snippet of action or a full scene. When footage is judged unsatisfactory by an on-the-spot decision, a *double take* is in order.

Erupting from lingo of the entertainment world, *double take* has come to mean anything deserving a second, or better, look.

DOUBLE-CROSS

In frontier America, a person unable to write was often required to sign a document. Under such circumstances, in lieu of a name it was legal to sign with an *X* on the form. Abraham Lincoln's mother followed this usage, along with multitudes of her contemporaries.

Often, a party to a contract agreed to the contract under pressure and didn't want to observe its terms. Oral lore insisted that when crosses were doubled, one being placed over the other, the first was cancelled or made null. Primitive as it sounds in the computer age, this *double-cross* was common enough to give its name to any act of deception or betrayal.

DRAW THE LINE

A game that was the ancestor to tennis involved hitting a ball back and forth across a net. It required little equipment, since players used their hands to strike that ball.

Precise dimensions for the court had not been established, so play could take place almost anywhere. Having selected a level spot, contestants stretched a net. Then each stepped an agreed distance from the net and drew a line that was the visual boundary.

For decades, players knocked balls back and forth in impromptu courts. Through influences of the game, the act of *drawing a boundary line* came to name the establishment of a limit of any kind.

DRIVER'S SEAT

Drivers of buggies and coaches made fun of persons who ventured to try self-propelled vehicles. "Get a horse!" was often shouted to the driver of a stalled car.

By 1912, opinion was changing rapidly. It was clear that anyone behind the steering wheel of a car was in a seat of awesome power. Never before had anyone had fingertip control of power greater than that of a forty-mule team.

In a new and important sense, the fate of a fast vehicle and its occupants rested with one person. Many kinds of drivers had occupied a great variety of seats for thousands of years. Yet it was the *driver's seat* of an automobile or truck that caused the position to name a person in charge of any enterprise.

DUCKS IN A ROW

Primitive versions of modern bowling were known many centuries ago. Pins of varied sizes and shapes were employed. Eventually they were standardized at fifteen inches in both height and circumference.

Originally called *ten-pins*, the equipment used in Europe was employed in the earliest American bowling saloons. The game was modified by introduction of a short, slender pin that was compared with a duck and, by extension, called a *duckpin*.

So many people reset so many pins in rows that one who completes a task is commended as having put his *ducks in a row*.

DUD

Anything can fail. Consequently, any enterprise ranging from an amateur play to an offering of high-priced homes around a golf course can be a *dud*.

Pioneer aviators who ushered the world into the era of aerial bombing saw their targets burst open at times. Often an explosive charge was delivered precisely, but a defective fuse caused it to have no effect except a dull thud. The instant a bomb hit, an experienced pilot knew whether or not it was a *dud*.

So many *duds* hit enemy positions without exploding that the term born in World War I came to designate any failure or ineffective action.

DUMBBELL

During the late Middle Ages, bell ringing was a highly regarded art. Men spent years learning to "ring the changes" on bells of great cathedrals. In its simplest standard form, this exercise called for a precise pattern of 5,040 notes played on seven bells. Since learners practiced for hours at a time for days on end, their noise was a public nuisance.

An unknown craftsman devised an elaborate rope mechanism to be used by apprentice ringers. The ringers went through all the motions but pulled *dumb* bells—counter-balanced weights or noise-less bells—rather than real ones. A workout with these instruments gave one plenty of exercise. So when an early health faddist invented a wooden apparatus for taking exercise, he named it the *dumbbell*.

DYED-IN-THE-WOOL

Any Technicolor movies set in the Middle Ages that show the characters in a variety of brightly colored costumes are lacking historical accuracy, for modern chemical dyes date from the 1700s. In earlier periods, even members of royalty wore comparatively drab clothing.

With few exceptions, dyes were of vegetable origin, and they seldom retained their brilliance through many washings. This was especially true of woolen clothing, which was likely to be blotched and uneven at the moment it was taken from the dye vat.

Some artisan made a revolutionary discovery that led to dyeing raw wool instead of garments or bolts of cloth. Colors were much more firmly fixed than earlier, and fabric made of dyed wool had a uniform appearance. As a result, it became customary to praise such goods as *dyed-in-the-wool*, and in time the phrase came to stand for unchanging in general.

EAGER BEAVER

If you plunge into a task or show enthusiasm, someone is likely to call you an *eager beaver*.

That admiring title, says folklore, comes from watching colonies of beavers at work. Some started gnawing trees and slapping mud into crevices with their tails right after sunup, frontiersmen swore. According to the same unimpeachable source, others took their own sweet time about joining the dam-building gang.

Observation by biologists has demolished this myth. There's no such thing as a beaver that's spectacularly eager. All members of rodent colonies are more or less alike—hard-working and skilled, but not markedly different in pace.

Realization that the four-footed eager beaver doesn't exist has not diminished the impact of the rhyming title. Often with admiration, sometimes with disgust, it is applied to any two-footed animal that seems more than eager to get started.

EAR TO THE GROUND

No region in the world has stimulated more red-blooded fiction than the American West. The Native American figures in these stories to such an extent that he has become a stock character in modern literature. He is a superb hunter and a fearless warrior. Untouched by civilization, he has developed his senses to an amazing degree. For example, he hears so well that when he suspects the approach of an enemy, he puts his ear to the ground and listens for the sound of men or horses. Especially in stony regions, he can readily determine just how many are coming and how far away they are.

There is no evidence that Native Americans ever listened for a footfall a mile or so away. Fiction writers made so many allusions to the practice that by 1900 it was familiar to every reader of pioneer yarns. Consequently, a person who listens for faint noises or watches for signs of a change in public sentiment is said to have an *ear to the ground.*

EASY STREET

Any time you find that a new acquaintance is living quite comfortably, you may think to yourself that he or she is living on *Easy Street.*

This expression sounds as though it might have come from Bunyan, Dickens, or Thackeray. It is not difficult to picture a broad avenue bearing this name, perhaps located not far from London's famous Grub Street.

Oddly, though, the designation originated in the New World. It seems to have first appeared in print in a 1902 novel entitled *It's Up to You,* one of whose more-than-prosperous characters "could walk up and down Easy Street."

It seems logical to describe a person in comfortable circumstances as having an address that summarized his or her lifestyle. The expression from the popular novel caught on, and *Easy Street* was soon widely familiar.

EAT ONE'S HAT

Many a man engaged in a contest of some sort has offered to eat his hat if he loses. In such a situation, a knowledge of etymology would be of great value—for the expression *eat one's hat* once referred not to a Stetson or a Panama, but to a culinary product.

Napier's famous *Boke of Cookry,* one of the earliest European cookbooks, gives the following directions: "Hattes are made of eggs, veal, dates, saffron, salt, and so forth." In the hands of amateur cooks, the concoction was frequently so unpalatable that it required a strong stomach to eat it.

Even so, the early braggart who offered to eat a *hatte* had in mind nothing so distasteful as a felt or a straw.

EGGS BENEDICT

Legend suggests that Saint Benedict is responsible for the combination of foods that seem to bear his name. Oral tradition long current in greater New York City credits the term to wealthy Samuel Benedict, about whom little is known.

Many scholars say that neither the saint nor the New Yorker had anything to do with creating and naming the perennially popular dish.

Instead, they say, it stems directly form the culinary interest of banker-yachtsman E. C. Benedict. He inherited a Connecticut fortune and reached the zenith of his power in commercial circles about the turn of the century.

It was on his yacht, says an account that stems from about 1902, that Benedict insisted that hollandaise sauce be added to the long-standard poached eggs on toast with ham. When a guest tried the new delicacy, he took to it like a duck to water. As a result, we still use the water-loving banker's name to designate the dish that is high on the list of favorite foods.

ELBOWROOM

Many British soldiers and Hessian mercenaries who fought under General John Burgoyne had one thing in common: they despised the aristocratic commander whose peers knew him as Gentleman Johnny.

According to a story dating from the time of the American Revolution, Burgoyne was much better at bragging than at fighting. Arriving in the vast region he was sent to subdue, he boasted that he would have plenty of *elbowroom* in which to operate. His remark, says legend, caused *elbowroom* to become a label for a maximum of space. That makes a story good enough to appear in more than one reputable source. But it's hard to believe that a single casual remark could have such lasting impact.

What could be more natural than to say that an area adequate for work or leisure gives a person room to move the elbows? As a term for a maximum of space, *elbowroom* was in use two centuries before Burgoyne's birth. That makes it highly improbable that Gentleman Johnny had anything to do with the fact that we continue to use this expression today.

ELEVENTH HOUR

Influenced by the Babylonians, Greeks and Hebrews adopted the use of sundials whose faces were divided into twelve segments. Hours were counted from daylight to dusk, with darkness coming at the twelfth. A famous New Testament parable (Matthew 20:1–16) expresses the idea of lateness by saying some would-be laborers came at the eleventh hour of sunlight.

Western civilization later modified timekeeping so that twelve o'clock came to mark both noon and midnight. That means the sun is hardly halfway across the heavens at eleven o'clock in the morning and has disappeared by that hour at night.

Force of the New Testament story is such that we still borrow from it. Despite the real position of the sun at the time, we continue to say that the *eleventh hour* is the last possible time to make a decision or to take action.

E-MAIL

The transmission of messages by government-operated and private mail services helped usher the Western world into the technological age. First letters and packages moved by surface mail, followed by telegrams, telephone messages, and airmail. Yet the old term for material sent through a postal system did not experience radical changes until hi-tech instruments became commonplace and inexpensive.

Development of recording devices that can be attached to

telephones produced voice mail—now omnipresent and a nuisance to some. Once it became possible for one computer to communicate with another computer, electronic mail surged into prominence. Strictly speaking, *e-mail* should be called something else since it doesn't flow through a postal system. New as the terminology is, however, academicians aren't likely to affect the increasingly important role of *e-mail*.

END OF ONE'S ROPE

Europeans invented and used a number of elaborate devices designed to give a horse freedom to graze but not to run away. Intricate hobbles and tethers seldom proved more effective than a length of rope, however.

With one end of a rope fastened to the bridle and the other to a post, a rider could rest while his mount filled its stomach. Many an animal moved to the end of the rope, then strained to eat grass barely within reach.

Like a tethered horse, a human who has exhausted all resources is at the *end of his or her rope*.

FACE THE MUSIC

If you are known to be ready to *face the music*, take it as a compliment—of sorts. Chances are that when facing an unpleasant or difficult situation, you grit your teeth and wade into it.

That is exactly what an old-time soldier who was being dismissed had to do. In his case, there was no choice. After being handed his walking papers, a deserter or slacker was made to march slowly between ranks of former comrades. Drums and other instruments marked time for this "rogue's march." Even though the situation offered no choice, it meant meeting the unpleasant head-on.

Today, a person who decides to *face the music* may be innocent of wrongdoing—but ready to act as bravely as a fellow who knew he was likely never to see comrades again.

FACE-OFF

Anticipating a confrontation and maybe hoping to avoid it, a person can get involved in a *face-off*. This situation doesn't demand the presence of notables; it can develop between next-door neighbors or a pair of fellow workers.

Chalk this expression up to sports, rather than to meetings between world leaders.

As the start of a hockey game approaches, two players face one another, tensed and poised. Each hopes to control the puck when an official drops it between them. This hostile situation leads us to label any confrontation as a *face-off*.

FALL GUY

Late in the last century, professional wrestling made a sudden spurt in popularity. Grunt-and-groan men fanned out from metropolitan areas and scheduled matches in dozens of small cities, often at agricultural expositions and county fairs.

Many, if not most, of the matches were fixed. One wrestler would agree to take a fall for a stipulated sum. His opponent would promise to handle him gently. But in order to make a match look good, the winner was often quite rough with the fellow who took the fall.

In sporting circles, it became common to speak of a loser as a *fall guy*. Firmly fixed in American speech by 1900, the sports expression came to indicate any loser, victim, or dupe.

FALLOUT

Physicists who developed and tested early atomic explosives were a long way from fully understanding what they were doing. The power of a blast was obvious and measurable, but it took only a few experiments to discover unexpected aftereffects.

When the bomb was dropped on Hiroshima, Japan, much of the city was leveled. Simultaneously, minute particles of radioactive material went high into the air. Some were blown downwind for many miles before they fell to the Earth's surface days later. In time, scientists learned that such fallout could be extremely dangerous or even lethal.

A situation may not really be over when it seems that it is. Sometimes there is *fallout*—aftereffects not anticipated at the time of the explosion.

FAR CRY

In medieval Scotland, petty kings were accustomed to publicizing their edicts by means of criers. These men went from place to place, shouting the terms of royal proclamations. Some announcements were local, applying to a single town or district. A courier entrusted with a message of that sort was said to be given a *near cry*.

In time of war or other national emergency, a crier might have to ride for days to complete his tour of duty. Such a *far cry* involved distances greater than the average man's travels of a lifetime. Hence, *far cry* came to be used as a synonym for "remote."

FARFETCHED

In some respects, the fifteenth and sixteenth centuries were among the most colorful of modern times. This was the age of exploration and adventure. New continents were being discovered; strange people and incredible beasts were being found.

All sorts of exotic things were brought back to Europe by sailors and explorers. Odd yellow tubers, called potatoes, came from the West Indies. Parrots were imported from Africa and tobacco from Virginia. Because such curiosities were fetched from afar, they were termed *farfetched*. In 1583, a London merchant slyly suggested to his customers that "far-fetched and dearly bought is good for ladies."

Adventurers brought home fantastic tales as well as strange objects. Some of them described an altogether unbelievable animal they called the kangaroo. Others told about land, people, and animals that have never existed, for this was the golden age of travel fiction. After being at sea a few months, a man could come home with a pack of fantastic lies and find someone gullible enough to swallow them. So many tales fetched from afar were proved false that any improbable report came to be labeled *farfetched*, or extremely unlikely.

FAST LANE

Until the automobile changed the nature and pace of society, no one talked about life in the *fast lane*.

Builders of the New Jersey Turnpike, two lanes wide in both directions, had a revolutionary idea from the start. Traffic would flow much more freely, they suggested, if slow-moving vehicles were required to stay in the right lane.

Experiments showed that the concept was correct, and it soon became standard practice for fast-moving vehicles—initially cars only—to use the left lane. Highway practices spawned talk about life in the *fast lane*, which now has come to refer to any high-stress situation that involves moving faster than one's comfort zone.

FATHOM

A *fathom*, the standard nautical measurement of depth, is six feet. The word comes from the Saxon *faethm* (outstretched arms). An act of Parliament once defined the term as "the length of a man's arms around the object of his affections." Contemporary usage of *fathom* generally refers to the capacity of a person to grasp an idea or concept—in a sense, how far they can "wrap their arms around" that idea or concept in trying to understand it.

FEATHER IN ONE'S CAP

Until modern times, ornamental feathers were more widely used by males than by females. Princes and noblemen vied with one another in finding colorful and expensive plumage with which to adorn their hats. Robin Hood, the prince of English outlaws, wouldn't have been seen in public without his feathers. Ostrich feathers constituted the special insignia of each Prince of Wales.

An unknown military leader hit upon the idea of using small feathers in lieu of badges of honor made by craftsmen. When a fighting man showed unusual gallantry, he was given a feather to wear in his cap.

By the time use of plumage was abandoned, language had been permanently affected. As a result, an honor or achievement of any kind is still called a *feather in one's cap*.

FEATHER ONE'S NEST

Four centuries ago, when this expression came into vogue in England, it was considered complimentary. Anyone who has ever watched a chickadee or a pair of wrens at work is conscious that the preparation of a nest is a big job. In order to be properly padded for babies, the nest must be lined with lots of feathers—not just a few.

Some birds are relatively sloppy builders; many are meticulous. One feather at a time is laid in place, often over a period of weeks. Well before the nest is ready for eggs, it is a marvel of craftsmanship directed toward a single goal—the welfare of babies.

It's true, of course, that some humans have little or no regard for colleagues. Such persons may *feather their own nests* without giving a thought to anyone else. But in the world of humans as well as that of flying folk, it isn't a bad idea to feather your nest as preparation for things to come. In modern usage, to *feather one's nest* usually has a financial connotation related to how well one is able to set himself or herself up in terms of savings, retirement plans, bank accounts, and so on.

FEELING ONE'S OATS

American frontiersmen found natural grasses so abundant that few of them bothered to sow grain. Only racehorses and the favorite mounts of landed aristocrats were stall-fed. Naturally, high mettle was a characteristic of blooded animals that had good food, plenty of exercise, and little hard work. Many horsemen ignored other factors and attributed such spirits to diet. Thus in 1843, the Canadian humorist Thomas Haliburton used the expression *feeling one's oats* to mean full of pep and high spirits and showing off.

FEET OF CLAY

Nebuchadnezzar II was the Babylonian king who captured Jerusalem in 587 BC, destroyed the city, and took the Hebrew people into captivity, ending the Judean kingdom. The Old Testament tells of his bouts of insanity when he imagined he was an ox and would go into the fields to eat grass.

The book of Daniel tells how the young Hebrew captive explained one of the king's strange dreams. Nebuchadnezzar had seen a giant image with a golden head, silver arms and breast, brass thighs, and iron legs. Every part was metal except the feet, which were compounded partly of iron and partly of potter's clay. Daniel said that his feet made the metal figure vulnerable, meaning that Babylon would be broken into pieces.

Impressed by this dramatic story, English readers of the Bible seized upon the weak spot of the strange figure as a symbol of weakness in general. Today, any noted person with a vulnerable point is still said to have *feet of clay*.

FEISTY

Some persons, more or less lethargic by nature, hardly know how to make a comeback for a slight or a slur. Others, just the opposite, are so *feisty* that they seem to go about looking for opportunities to engage in spats and pick quarrels.

Members of the second category may not consider themselves dogged, but if speech means anything, they're like some four-footed critters. For in the highly specialized language of southern dialect, any quick-tempered lapdog is a *fice*.

At least in times past, the owner of a fice was likely to give it the best of food and a lot of attention. No wonder one of these pampered little animals was likely to have a temper with a short fuse!

Fice-like attitudes and reactions on the part of two-legged creatures warrants use of the label *feisty*—an indirect way of suggesting that a person is as snappy as a poodle.

FERRET OUT

One of the strangest animals brought to Europe by Crusaders who had been in Africa made a good pet. But the newcomer to England and Europe was so fond of eggs that it was often caught stealing them. From a corruption of an old expression used to describe "a thief with fur," the egg stealer came to be known as the *ferret*.

Easily trained, the pink-eyed imported animal was widely used to hunt rats. Eventually it became both a serious pursuit and a popular sport to ferret for rabbits and other burrowing animals.

Charles Dickens's imagination was fired by the egg stealer's name, so he picked it up and applied it to detective work. As a result, we say that a searcher for hidden things—not necessarily underground—is busy *ferreting out* secrets.

FIASCO

Long ago, Venice became a great center of the glass trade. Her craftsmen developed the now standard goblet made up of bowl, stem, and foot. They also imitated semiprecious stones in the color and texture of fine ware. Many pieces were so prized that royal inventories listed them along with gold and silver vessels.

In addition to costly ware, Italian artisans produced great quantities of the common flask—which in some dialects was known as a *fiasco*.

Flaws frequently developed in the process of turning out fine pieces. Glass was too expensive to throw away; even damaged, a hunk of it could be reheated and turned into a fiasco or two. So many inexpensive flasks were the result of bungling that the glass blower's term came to indicate any type of failure.

At least, that is maybe the most believable of half a dozen theories offered to account for the rise of a distinctive and elusive word.

FIELD DAY

Once in a while everyone ought to enjoy a *field day*. It makes little or no difference what goings-on are involved; romping around and having things pretty much as you want them is a special kind of self-rewarding activity.

That is what members of fraternities, sororities, and civic clubs discovered long ago. Instead of sticking strictly to routine, many groups of this nature announced that two weeks from Saturday every member would spend the day outdoors. Rivals were challenged to set the day aside, too, in order to compete in games and sports.

Canny leaders often arranged things so that it would be difficult or impossible for a really tough set of opponents to be on hand at the time selected. This meant that sponsors could cavort through the *field day*, having things their own way and gloating at winning easy victories.

FIFTH WHEEL

Every few years, you see a story about an inventor who has come up with a way to turn tap water into gasoline. So far, no chemical or gadget has made a dent in the revenue of OPEC countries.

Long before gasoline became a necessity of life, opportunists took advantage of persons always on the go. All sorts of contrivances were touted as adding efficiency or comfort to surreys and broughams and carriages.

One widely sold device was a horizontal wheel attachment to the front axle of a vehicle. Sometimes it provided a little support and stability during sharp turns. On good roads, however, this fifth wheel was a useless addition.

Except for the benefit of tourists, fifth wheels of this sort—and vehicles that sport them—are long gone. Their influence was great enough, though, to form a jocular label for a person who rolls along partnerless with a group.

FIGHT FIRE WITH FIRE

Fire was a fearful foe of householders on the American frontier. Most cabins were built in small clearings, but grass and brush might extend nearly to the doors. Disaster threatened whenever flames, pushed by the wind, approached. In this situation, settlers often set backfires. This meant burning a strip in the path of a big blaze, then extinguishing the fire to leave barren ground that would not burn. To *fight fire with fire* was a desperate venture, for the control strip might get out of hand and add to the danger instead of reducing it. Consequently, the frontier term has come to indicate any emergency measure that involves great hazard.

FIGUREHEAD

Many early ships were painted or carved to display creatures designed to frighten sailors on enemy vessels. Such symbols were replaced by human figures placed over the cut-water when cannons made ships genuinely threatening.

A carved representation of a ship owner or nobleman was often the figure near the head of a big vessel. HMS *Marlborough*, a British warship, had as its figurehead "the Great Duke"—complete with long, curling hair and medals on his chest.

During the great age of sail, figureheads of many vessels were conventional representations of Victorian women. Such a carved dummy at the prow looked important but played no role in the ship's operation.

Today, lots of persons with important-sounding titles have no authority to make decisions. "Only a *figurehead*," say insiders who regard such a man or woman as being a lot like a wooden dummy.

FIRE-EATER

In many cultures, people have experimented with swallowing smoke and flames. European showmen of the seventeenth century managed to convince onlookers that they actually ate glowing coals.

Keen interest in the exploits of the *fire-eaters* who flourished in that era led to wide use of their name in other circumstances. It was initially applied to bullies who were so fond of fighting that they willingly faced danger. Later the term was associated with any person quick and eager to work—going at it with the relish a performer showed in eating fire.

FIRESTORM

A single sentence, less than carefully delivered, can unleash a *firestorm* of criticism in the aftermath of a presidential press conference. So can a decision by an executive or a member of the family, for that matter.

In such instances, reaction is quick and furious. Even though only words may be involved, destruction can be awesome. Which is why the term that took shape during war is appropriate for use in many civilian situations.

Wave after wave of planes dropped incendiary bombs on enemy cities before Allied forces achieved victory during World War II. Triggered by aerial bombing and spreading so rapidly that there was no way on earth to stop it, a firestorm could wreak havoc comparable to that caused by an atomic bomb.

These highly specialized missiles once used in great quantities have been made all but obsolete by more sophisticated weapons. But the *firestorm* set off by tons of incendiaries lives on in speech as a memorial, of sorts, to the raging destruction it symbolizes.

FIRST RATE

During the heyday of her naval expansion, Britain set up an elaborate system of classification. Every warship she owned was inspected and placed in a category, or rate, which was determined by the number and weight of the guns she mounted. There were six of these rates, and members of the Royal Navy measured their prestige by the rate of their vessel. Every officer hoped to command, some day, a ship of the first rate. Standing as it did for the mightiest vessels afloat, *first rate* came to be used for anything high in quality, whether on sea or land.

FIRST-STRING

First-string and *second-string,* expressions familiar on every athletic field, originated when archery was the chief sport. Around the thirteenth century, the five-foot English longbow became the world's most formidable weapon. At Abergavenny in 1182, a Welsh archer using a longbow of yew shot an arrow through a four-inch oak slab. Ordinary armor was no defense against it.

Royal proclamations urged adoption of the weapon, and in 1363 Edward III made it mandatory for men to engage in contests with the longbow on every Sunday and holiday.

These meets were the chief sporting events of the times, and every man coveted a prize. Much of the marksman's success lay in the use of a good bowstring. Although an archer usually had several strings, he invariably had a favorite that he considered superior to his others. In Middle English speech this was his *fyrst-streng*. When firearms made the longbow obsolete, the expression for one's finest bowstring became attached to the best squad in any group of contestants, so *secounde-streng* was a logical successor to *first-string*.

FIT AS A FIDDLE

In one form or another, the stringed fiddle was popular in England nearly a thousand years ago. Sizes and shapes varied, as did the number and length of strings.

All early fiddles were handmade, and most were used in rural settings. Listeners, as well as players, knew when the tension of the strings was not right or when an instrument was warped. Only an undamaged one that was properly adjusted was in top shape, or fit to use with an audience.

Hundreds of years later, a person in vigorous good health is still said to be as *fit as a fiddle*—undamaged, and well-tuned, that is.

FLASH IN THE PAN

Early Americans hunted game under conditions that would baffle many modern hunters. Their greatest handicap was the inefficiency of crude flintlock guns. When a trigger was snapped, friction between flint and steel might produce a good spark—or might yield none.

Even a strong spurt of flame didn't guarantee that a gun would fire. It was equipped with a shallow pan in which a trail of powder led from flint to charge. A jolt or a period of dampness could render the thin line of powder ineffective. In such cases, the flash of light from the pan was not followed by detonation of a charge. Such a *flash in the pan* was experienced so frequently that we use the weapon's reference to stand for any quick and dazzling failure.

FLIP SIDE

Chinese think and speak of the working of opposite cosmic forces in terms of yin and yang. Americans, more versed in technology than in philosophy, say that every argument and each set of principles has a *flip side.*

Though the expression is too firmly entrenched in speech to face an early demise, the technology that produced it is virtually obsolete. Tape cassettes wreaked havoc in the phonograph record industry; compact discs have sounded its death knell.

But in its heyday, the revolving platter ruled popular music in the Western world. Practically every song that went through the top of the charts was accompanied by another that didn't rival it in popularity. Cut into the reverse face of a record, this musical hitchhiker was noticeably different from its companion, which meant that practically every record had its *flip side*—a second recording that gave listeners a quite different impression from that produced by the first.

FLY OFF THE HANDLE

If you've ever seen a person *fly off the handle*, you might have been impressed by the energy and speed involved with that eruption of anger.

Frontiersmen found it hard to control their tempers when tools suddenly failed them. A common cause of such a turn of events was the shrinkage of wood—universally used for tool handles.

After having hung in a shed for months, the handle of a hoe or a rake was likely to come off after a few strokes. In the case of an ax, badly worn or shrunken wood is positively dangerous because the head of the tool can come loose at the first lick.

When the blade of an ax flies off the handle, it endangers the user and everyone standing nearby. That makes it almost as great a source of danger as a violent explosion of temper.

FORK OVER

Noblemen owned most of Britain's good farmland until modern times. Peasants who wanted to rent were required to promise to pay in silver.

At harvest time, landlords sent collection agents for the annual rent—often before crops could be sold. A tenant without silver had to make payment in kind with his produce.

Shrewd agents often allowed less than market value for grain or other staples accepted in lieu of silver. So a farmer forced to deliver his rent with a pitchfork cursed under his breath while making his payment.

Today, substitutions for money are rarely, if ever, accepted. Also, a person is more likely to *fork over* greenbacks to a creditor or a bookie than to a landlord of noble birth.

FRAZZLED

Anytime you confess to being *frazzled*, you compare yourself with the frayed end of a rope.

At least as early as the era in which Britain was busy establishing colonies in North America, sailors had special words for kinds and conditions of their all-important ropes.

A length of hemp that had seen considerable use, but could be repaired, was *frayed*. In many cases, damage went so far that a section had to be cut off before the shortened rope could be used again. Such a piece of disheveled hemp was so much like the body and mind of an absolutely exhausted person that both came to be called *frazzled*.

FREELANCE

Does your circle of acquaintances include a *freelance* artist or writer? Or maybe a musician or tax preparer?

Whatever his or her field of activity may be, the modern freelancer is not on a payroll. Instead, services or products are offered directly to purchasers—often without a middle man.

The *lance* part of *freelance* harks back to the Middle Ages when knights fought with sword and lance. Most warriors had sworn allegiance to the king or lord of their realm. Others were roving soldiers or medieval mercenaries who operated on their own, offering their swords, lances, and services to the highest bidder. Freebooters arose a few centuries later, and these fellows outfitted their own ships in order to prowl the seas. Today, we call them pirates.

The term *freelance* was popularized by the novel *Ivanhoe*, published in 1819. Oddly enough, the book was written by a knight, Sir Walter Scott. *Ivanhoe* brought to us a term that is more poetic and versatile than "self-employed person."

FREELOADER

At every old-fashioned picnic sponsored by a church or a lodge or a community, a few zealous people did more than their share of the work. When the food was spread, such a gathering was sure to attract at least one person who brought along nothing but a tremendous appetite.

A man, woman, or half-grown child who loaded his or her stomach with free food was usually tolerated but was not urged to come back the following year. Invited or not, such a person was likely to show up again, even more hungry than the last time

Soon the *freeloader* became a stock character, always present where there was something to eat. Spawned at the picnic table, the title transferred to any sponger or moocher who is a conspicuous consumer but doesn't contribute to expenses.

FREE-WHEELER

Immense amounts of capital backed the original *free-wheeler* of the highways. During the 1930s, a drawing board wizard outlined plans for a brand-new kind of car. Built with capacity to coast freely without being slowed by the engine, it was touted as capable of putting the competition out of business.

Several versions of the free-wheeler went on the market and were briefly sensational. Then it was found that there are serious drawbacks to fast movement by the force of gravity alone. So many sets of brakes were burned out and so many cars crashed that automakers returned to the time-honored practice of linking wheels with motors.

Abandoned by Detroit, the *free-wheeler* survives in language as a tribute, of sorts, to what some engineers consider benighted genius.

FREUDIAN SLIP

Maybe you keep such close watch of your tongue that you've never, never made a *Freudian slip*. If so, you're practically in a class by yourself. From time to time, most of us blurt out something that seems to reveal thoughts we prefer to hide.

Such verbal self-exposure owes its worldwide use and name to the founder of psychoanalysis.

Austrian neurologist Sigmund Freud was still studying in Paris at age thirty. Once he began seeing patients, however, he started developing new theories. Soon he said that every abnormal mental state involves repressed memories. Dreams, he reported in a sensational turn-of-the-century book, stem largely from repressed sexual desires.

Anyone interviewed by the great doctor or one of his early disciples was sure to say something that evoked an "Aha!" reaction from the analyst. That was inevitable, for everyday speech is saturated with sexual innuendoes and overtones.

A comment considered bland and innocent by a patient might be seen by Freud to indicate severe maladjustment. Hence any unplanned verbal revelation, not necessarily sexual now, is termed a *Freudian slip*.

FUNNY BONE

Human anatomy was largely a mystery until comparatively recent times. Because skeletons were abundant, bones were the first body parts to be the subject of scientific study. Terms were chosen from Latin because it was the universal language of scholarship.

There is no record of who first gave serious attention to the relatively big bone that runs from the shoulder to the elbow, but it is technically known as the *humerus* (which is Latin for "upper arm").

Some jokester framed a pun and called the tip of the humerus the *funny bone*. Bumping this bone is not humorous even to the persons unacquainted with classical languages. Yet it yields a distinctively unusual—or funny—sensation when struck against a hard surface.

GAGA

Next time you are going *gaga* over a singer, entertainer, or brand-new fashion, someone may suggest that you have suddenly gone wild about the work of French artist Paul Gauguin.

An old tale has it that early admirers of the painter had difficulty pronouncing his name. Struggling with it, they settled for repetition of the first syllable. People who were absolutely mad about Gauguin's work were derided as being *Ga-Ga*.

The only part of that story that is true is that the word is of French origin. Meaning "fool" or "old fool," the French used the word as an echo of the fool's mindless sounds.

GARBLE

Only a few substances that can be used to flavor foods are native to Europe. By the 1200s, spices were being imported from the Far East, and one of the chief centers of the trade was Alexandria, where cargoes were unloaded for resale to Western Europe. After the long journey by caravan across Asia, wholesale merchants had to go through each lot of spices to separate the good from the bad. In Arabic, this operation was called *gharbala* (to sift).

Then, no matter how carefully the sifting was done, seawater, mildew, and rot caused additional damage by the time the cargo reached Britain, where the process came to be known as *garble.*

By 1650 the term invaded the literary world. Persons were said to *garble* a religious or political paper when they selectively sifted out words to distort meaning. Obviously, such a procedure frequently muddled the meaning of the writer, so today the word means mixed-up or incomprehensible.

GET A BREAK

In pocket billiards, or pool, the first shot of the game is the most important. No matter where the first shot hits the balls that have been arranged in the form of a triangle, the orderly arrangement is broken.

Skilled players know how to break in such a fashion that the cue ball stops at an advantageous point. An especially good break can lead to a run of the table—every ball pocketed before an opponent has an opportunity to shoot.

Comparing any sudden advantage with a splendid first shot at the pool table, a person who receives a stroke of luck is said to *get a break.*

GET ONE'S GOAT

A family member or fellow worker who has learned what button to push may *get your goat* at the drop of a hat.

Stable attendants were long convinced that the best way to soothe a high-strung racehorse was to give the animal a little companion. Not just any companion, but a goat.

Once the horse became accustomed to the presence of the horned ruminant, it created an equine crisis to remove the stablemate. At least, that's the widespread oral tradition that offers to explain why a person who can make you angry or frustrated is said to *get your goat.*

GET THE BALL ROLLING

Croquet was one of England's favorite games during much of the nineteenth century. Annual matches at Wimbledon drew crowds that rivaled the size of those that now turn out for tennis tournaments.

One insurmountable liability contributed to its fall from favor: there is no way to organize a game so that each player has an equal chance to win. Given the first shot, an expert can often reach the goal before anyone else has had a chance to start.

Because of this factor, it is all-important to be the first player. A coin is often tossed to see who gets to begin. During the era when croquet was king of the lawn, a person who took charge of any beginning borrowed from the game and said he or she would *get the ball rolling.*

GIBBERISH

Early in the sixteenth century, villagers of England noticed that many swarthy foreigners were afoot. Since these strange folks had black hair and tawny skins, it was assumed that they came from Egypt. Though they were known for a time as Egyptians, common folk soon shortened their title to Gypsies. Always keeping their distance from others, close-knit bands of Gypsies perpetuated ancient customs.

Even their language was distinctive—to the English villagers, it seemed as if the dark-skinned Gypsies were jabbering pure nonsense. The English coined a special word, *gibberish*, to name such talk. Half a century after the title entered speech, it became associated with sound-imitating words such as *gibber* and *jabber*.

Firmly established in everyday speech, the title expanded, and we now use it to label any incoherent jumble of sounds.

GIG

Our earliest ancestors probably spent hundreds of generations learning to count as many objects as there were fingers on their hands. Even then, mastery of the abstract concept "ten" lay far in the future. Gradually moving upward in mathematical ability, humans learned to deal with hundreds and then with thousands. The ability to think or calculate in terms of millions came a great deal later.

Now, in the third millennium, the capacity to store, retrieve, and transmit electronic information has required another giant mathematical step since it's commonplace to think and to act in terms of billions of data units. The abbreviation of the classical Greek term for "gigantic" made it customary to use *giga* to indicate a binary billion, or ten to the ninth power. With the final letter dropped, it became a *gig*.

The development of gigabyte-capacity storage disks—actually equivalent to 1,024 megabytes—is now taken for granted.

GLOSS OVER

Religious, legal, and technical works have often included difficult words and phrases. Before printed books became abundant, it was customary to insert into a manuscript a *gloss*, or explanation, at each point where interpretation seemed difficult.

Many a gloss (from the Latin word meaning "explain" or "translate") actually clarified meaning, but some scholars who wrote between the lines or in the margins introduced meanings not consistent with the text. As a result, one who changed the meaning of a passage by means of marginal comments was said to *gloss over* it. Influenced by German, the term also acquired an additional meaning of giving a false interpretation or explanation. An early literary critic recorded his vexation at friends of a writer "who are tender of his fame and gloss over this foible by calling him an agreeable novelist." A modern sweetheart who has no notion of adding explanatory comments to a technical book may admit that he's prone to *gloss over* the faults of his lady love.

GO BANANAS

What makes a person who is normally calm and quiet suddenly *go bananas*? Why do we specify this fruit instead of Granny Smith apples or Bosc pears?

No one knows exactly why a person will go wacko in a given situation. But there's a good reason for saying that anyone temporarily out of control has gone bananas. Actions of such a person are a lot like that of a caged monkey in a zoo. The sight of a keeper approaching with a bunch of bananas can make the animal freak out, or *go bananas*.

GO TO POT

A person, business, or community can *go to pot* very rapidly. No person or enterprise is immune from the danger of taking a downward course named from household customs of long ago.

English squires of the fifteenth century ate much more meat than do most modern people. Beef was favored, but mutton and pork were also consumed in large quantities. After the best pieces were cut off a roasted joint, the remnant was likely to be used in making stew. This meant that it went into a pot along with potatoes, onions, and other vegetables.

Degeneration of all sorts came to be designated as *going to pot*—the description of the downward journey of a once splendid roast.

GOBLIN

Scholars are at odds concerning the origin of *goblin* as one name for a mischievous spirit. Some point to a twelfth-century literary work by Ordericus Vitalis, who mentioned Goblinus as the name of a ghost that haunted the town of Eureux. This reference, they say, created the word that was later abbreviated into today's form.

Not so, according to a host of critics who point out that *gobelin* wasn't regularly used until the sixteenth century. These scholars point out that a brilliant scarlet fabric unlike anything ever seen before appeared in Paris markets around 1435. Wealthy matrons vied with one another in buying tapestries made by Gilles and Jehan Gobelin, but some of their husbands frowned on the exotic cloth. It was so much more vivid in color than any previous red material that it was rumored the brothers had sold their souls to the devil in order to learn how to make the dye.

King Louis XIV made the Gobelin establishment a royal factory. Rivals denounced the craftsmen, however, and accused them of sorcery. Sentiment against the dyers was so widespread that common people began using their name as an expression for an evil spirit. As the years passed, one letter dropped from their name and the now-familiar *goblin* was formed.

GOES WITH THE TERRITORY

If you are offered a new job, it might be a good idea to ask what *goes with the territory*. Many times, a spot that looks tempting has requirements not immediately apparent that are less than desirable.

Since the first traveling salesman hit the road, that has been the case with people who choose this way to make a living. Few if any sales territories offer only plums; there is always at least one tough nut to crack and maybe a day or two of nearly impossible schedules.

Already widely recognized, the fact that something unpleasant *goes with the territory* was embedded in speech through the impact of Arthur Miller's hit play, *Death of a Salesman*.

GOOSE BUMPS

Any thrilling experience, from catching a glimpse of a movie star to attending the Kentucky Derby, may give you *goose bumps*.

Geese were important in the life of medieval Britain—so important that gooseherds spent their lives tending flocks. Many owners plucked their geese five times a year, leaving them totally naked until new feathers appeared. When cold air hit such a bird, tiny muscles just under the skin would contract and create patterns of pimples.

The plucking of geese for feathers was common in Yorkshire until late in the last century and is sometimes seen even today.

It doesn't take a draft to cause wee muscles of some humans to contract; emotion can do the job. Regardless of what triggers them into visibility, small and transient bumps on the human skin are so much like those of a plucked fowl that it's logical and natural to call them *goose bumps*.

GRANDSTAND PLAY

If a colleague or fellow citizen makes a *grandstand play*, it may bring publicity without affecting the outcome of an issue.

Long before baseball offered million-dollar contracts, players were popular heroes. Maybe because most accolades went to pitchers and batters, some fielders developed a way of attracting the attention of spectators. With a little practice, a fellow could learn to make an easy fielding play look as though it required a lot of skill and effort.

Such a maneuver had no effect on the final score. But it could be the talk of the town among fans who were thrilled by it. Enough dramatic stunts were pulled that *grandstand play* was adopted into general speech.

GRAVEYARD SHIFT

Every industry that operates around the clock has a *graveyard shift*. Some persons who punch a clock at odd hours think their time of work has some sort of connection with burial places. But the true origin is not quite so obvious.

Any thick liquid was called *gravy* for a long, long time. Only special kinds of gravy went on the table. "Humour running from the eyes" caused some people to be called *gravy-eyed*.

In addition to disease, late vigils in bed led to bleary eyes. Sailors who had the watch that started at midnight were often gravy-eyed before they went off duty. That led them to speak of the middle watch as the *gravey-eyed shift*.

Landlubbers who heard the expression didn't fully understand it. Aided by superstitions about cemeteries, the sea-born label became the *graveyard shift* in industry.

GRAVY TRAIN

If you go in for meat, you probably enjoy gravy. From pot roast to country ham, a cut can yield this by-product that may be tastier than the meat itself.

Gravy is an "extra," or bonus from cooking. So the name of the tongue-pleasing liquid is applied to anything gained without effort or cost. In the era when home-cooked gravy was most abundant, a favorite way to travel was by train. Many railroad workers began using *gravy train* to name a well-paid run that required little work.

During the financial boom of the 1920s, railroad lingo moved into financial circles to designate an undemanding position that paid a big salary.

Today, we call any easy job or activity that pays more than it seems to be worth a *gravy train*—nonedible and involving little or no movement.

GREASE ONE'S PALM

Most modern women spend more time and money on adornment of the body than do men, but for centuries the reverse was true. Kings, knights, and gallants of the Age of Chivalry prided themselves on their appearance as much as on their valor. Soap was almost unheard of, however, so doughty fellows made lavish use of perfumed and spiced goose grease. Charcoal was sometimes added to give the user's skin a fashionable dark glow.

Packed in membranes, such grease was so highly prized that it was often used as a gift when a favor was desired. Jokingly perhaps at first, a fellow who wished a concession from an official would offer him a gift of "grease for his palm." This usually took the form of gold or silver, so by the sixteenth century to *grease one's palm* was commonly used to designate bribery.

GREAT SCOTT!

Unless you read a great many novels set in the past, you aren't likely to exclaim "Great Scott!" when startled. But you'll find that phrase in the pages of many literary classics. It is there, some scholars believe, through influence of a long-time commander of the U.S. Army.

Vain Winfield S. Scott was disliked. Some subordinates resented the fact that he became a brigadier general and a brevet major general at age twenty-eight. Others claimed that he spent his time and energy strutting and swaggering instead of looking after his troops.

Nicknamed "Old Fuss and Feathers" before he ran for the presidency in 1852, he later became known as "Great Scott." Picked up by civilians, that title spawned the exclamation *Great Scott!* that punctuated speech during the Gay Nineties.

GUM UP THE WORKS

Veteran lumbermen who reached North America very early could hardly believe their eyes. It seemed impossible that a single continent could boast such a profusion and variety of fine trees. One of them, a sweet gum, stretched in a broad belt from Connecticut to Missouri and from Florida to Mexico. Now often called the red gum, the tree is still a major source of lumber.

Aside from its size and abundance, the gum interested pioneers because of its fragrant resin. Lumbermen didn't like the stuff since it clogged up their saws. But venturesome boys discovered it was pleasant to chew, so they frequently went on gumming expeditions. After gathering a quantity of the sticky stuff, a youngster was likely to be dabbed from head to foot. Gum was hard to wash from clothing and all but impossible to clean from hair.

Proverbial sayings came to include many references to the stuff. As a result, any person throwing a project into confusion is said to be *gumming up the works*.

GUNG HO

Many a *gung ho* sales trainer or sports fan manages to raise the level of enthusiasm of others. That is appropriate, since early usage of the ancient term involved groups of persons.

A few Europeans managed to get into China as soon as westerners began to be tolerated. All such visitors were awed by the Great Wall and other public works constructed by human labor. Big projects still under way employed vast numbers of coolies. At an overseer's signal, they shouted *"Gung ho!"* in unison in order to synchronize movements.

It became more popular in the West when it became a slogan adopted by the U.S. Marines under General E. Carlson in World War II. Less than fully understood, the Chinese phrase for "work together" was applied to actions of any enthusiast.

GYMNASIUM

By nearly every standard, the Greeks were the most enlightened people of ancient times. They even developed a program of physical education at public expense because they felt that physical training was essential. It was limited to males, and they trained and competed in the nude to maximize the freedom of movement.

So from *gymnos* (naked) the building in which they worked out was called a *gymnasion*. The Romans adopted both the building and the training program. With the efficiency for which they are famous, the Romans built many a new *gymnasion* so that their young men might be trained for sports and war. Even the profligate emperor Nero took interest in the program and gave a great central *gymnasion* to the city of Rome.

After the fall of the empire, the concept of physical education was forgotten for hundreds of years. Then, around the sixteenth century, English scholars rediscovered the classical word, and now *gymnasium* designates any building devoted to physical education.

HACKER

For centuries the verb *hack* has meant the action of cutting or chopping anything from stove wood to enemy soldiers by means of a series of short blows delivered by an ax, a sword, or some other blade.

Only a fraction of present-day Americans regularly go out to hack wood into pieces small enough to be burned in a stove. Hi-tech weapons have made battle-axes, swords, sabers, and all other sharp-edged, hand-wielded weapons obsolete. Yet the number of persons who spend time delivering repeated blows to electronic systems in order to understand or infiltrate them appears to be growing.

Today's *hacker* may spend days or weeks repeatedly striking a computer system for purposes of harm, mischief, or simple curiosity. Dedicated perseverance and use of the brain make a hacker a force to be reckoned with in the modern world.

HAIR-RAISING

As a synonym for "frightful," *hair-raising* is one of the most striking labels in modern speech. The term has been in use only a few generations. Pioneers and soldiers who fought the American Indians were horrified when they first learned that Indians scalped their victims, but early in American history whites also adopted the practice. Scalps of slain Indians were turned in when their killers wished to collect the bounty offered by authorities. Shaping a grim joke, Indian fighters began to speak of scalping as "lifting the hair" or "hair-raising."

This bloody practice was largely abandoned when peace treaties were signed with the Indians. Nevertheless, *hair-raising* had made so strong an impact upon speech that the term remained in the language to indicate an extremely frightful experience. Helped by association with reactions of startled dogs and cats, it's now applied to humans in spite of the fact that it has been thousands of years since ordinary persons may have had muscles that could pull their hair erect when frightened.

HALF-BAKED

Each type of bread or pastry not only has its special recipe of ingredients—it also must be baked at the proper temperature for the right length of time.

A person learning to bake is often afraid of burning his or her product. As a result, a beginner is likely to take bread out of the oven too soon. Once cooled and cut, it cannot be put back for additional baking.

Anyone or anything raw or incomplete or foolish is likely to be called *half-baked*—about as desirable as undercooked products of the oven.

HALF-COCKED

As late as the time of the American Revolution, the sportsmen of England shot game with heavy and clumsy muskets. Their weapons had to be loaded slowly by hand, for they wouldn't fire until cocked.

As a safety measure, many a musket was made so that it could be half-cocked. From that position, it took a less complex set of movements to get the weapon ready to fire.

Veteran hunters were careful to cock their muskets as soon as they came close to game. Beginners who hadn't learned to do this were likely to develop "buck fever" at the sight of a deer. While trying to fire from the half-cocked position, a fellow might see a coveted trophy scoot out of sight, unharmed.

Like an amateur hunter, a person failing to make final preparations before trying to launch an enterprise may be stymied as a result of having gone off *half-cocked*.

HAND OVER FIST

Rope ladders leading to main spars of many sailing vessels made it easy to climb into the rigging. When a gale blew up suddenly, a captain might order men aloft at top speed. Once canvas was furled, men needed to get on deck quickly in order to avoid being tossed overboard when the ship lurched. Rope ladders were too clumsy for such descent. It was customary for a man to grab a big rope and then climb down hand over hand.

Speed of such descent caused any rapid progress to be labeled *hand-over-hand*. Influenced by popularity of boxing in the eighteenth century, the expression was modified to *hand over fist*.

Steamships quickly made the hand over fist descent of a rope obsolete, but the expression was firmly fixed in speech. A curious twist of fate led to inversion of its original sense. Today, a person who ascends the business world rapidly is likely to be described as making money *hand over fist*.

HANDICAP

Sixteenth-century English gamblers had little equipment for organized games of chance. Decks of playing cards were available only to the wealthy, and dice were scarce and expensive. Ordinary fellows therefore developed a gambling game that required no equipment other than a hat or cap. A fellow wishing to get up a game would offer to trade some article with an acquaintance. For example, he might suggest exchanging his hood for another's cloak. Since no two articles were of identical worth, traders would select an umpire to decide the cash difference.

All three men dropped forfeit money into a cap, and the traders held their hands over the money. Then the umpire announced his decision concerning the difference in the value of the articles involved. With their eyes closed, the hagglers removed their hands from the cap—fists open or closed to indicate acceptance or refusal of the umpire's terms. If both agreed to trade or not to trade, forfeit money went to the umpire; otherwise, it went to the man who accepted the umpire's decision. Each of the three men stood to lose two ways and win in only one way, so a fellow with a *hand in cap* took considerable risk.

Then horse racers began using umpires to stipulate weights to be carried, and the term was shortened from *hand in cap* to *handicap*. By the eighteenth century, the meaning had expanded to include any type of weight, encumbrance, disadvantage, or disability.

HANDS DOWN

Anytime you score a victory without effort, you will win *hands down*—even if your hands were waving above your head at the moment of the finish.

Though firmly established, the origin for this phrase meaning an easy triumph is not clear. Some horsemen vow that it stems from the fact that a jockey may find his horse way out in front of the pack. That means the rider doesn't even have to lift his hands in order to guide his mount to a win.

Another theory gets *hands down* from the boxing ring. A prizefighter occasionally gets matched with a pushover. In such a bout, the stronger and more expert contender waltzes to victory after having barely raised his fists a few times.

You can pay your money and take your pick: a horse race that practically ends in a canter or ten rounds in a ring during which the winner never works up a sweat. Either way, one contender will win *hands down*.

HAND-TO-MOUTH

In 1586, Great Britain experienced a failure of grain crops. Thousands starved during a period of famine, and multitudes who survived became thin from hunger. Food was often so scarce that when a person managed to get a bit, he behaved like Kurdish refugees in twentieth-century Iraq. As soon as a person had a piece of bread in his hand, he would thrust it into his mouth to make sure no one would snatch it away.

Hand-to-mouth existence was a fact of life until modern times. So many persons practiced it that we still use the phrase to label substandard living conditions.

HANDWRITING ON THE WALL

Ancient Babylon flourished under the rule of King Nebuchadnezzar, but his son and successor, Belshazzar, proved weak and profligate. Ignoring all standards, he once drank heavily from holy vessels seized from the Temple of Jerusalem. A mysterious hand appeared after this act of sacrilege and to the astonishment of the king wrote four strange words on the wall of the banquet room.

Only the Hebrew prophet, Daniel, could interpret the mysterious message. He boldly told the ruler that they spelled disaster for him and for his nation. Soon afterward Belshazzar was defeated and slain, just as Daniel said.

Religious dramas of the Middle Ages often included vivid interpretations of events in the ancient banquet hall. Viewers of such pageants sat enthralled as they watched the writing of the strange warning to a king. As a result, any threat of impending doom is still known as *handwriting on the wall*.

HANKY-PANKY

What on earth leads us to say that a person fooling around on a mate or other underhanded business is engaged in *hanky-panky*? Strange as it seems, the expression is a logical one whose roots are easily traced.

In many eras, magicians learned to keep the eyes of observers off their doings by means of distraction. An umbrella or a coffin is a tried-and-proven source, as is a handkerchief for that matter.

About 150 years or so ago, many a British master of fast movements swung a handkerchief with one hand to keep viewers from noticing what he was doing with the other. This practice was so common that use of a hanky came to be associated with clandestine activity. Maybe influenced by *hocus-pocus,* a rhyming word was added.

Presto! Quicker than you can bat your eyes, *hanky-panky* came into being as just the right label for undercover doings.

HARD-BOILED

Hard-boiled persons get their title—not from likeness to a cooked egg, but from washday habits of American pioneers. Homemakers of frontier days used lye soap and often washed in an open stream. Clothes tended to gray very quickly, so at least once a month the fastidious woman boiled her wash in a black iron pot. Then she starched the best pieces with a paste made in her own kitchen.

She sometimes got her husband's Sunday shirts too stiff. Trying to make the best of the situation, he would jokingly accuse his wife of having boiled the clothes so long they became hard. Passing from stiffly starched clothing, the colorful term attached to people, and the *hard-boiled* American emerged as a callous, unfeeling, tough person.

HARROWING

Long before Columbus discovered America, European farmers were using a heavy wooden frame equipped with many sharp teeth. Dragged over plowed ground, a harrow uprooted weeds while pulverizing the soil.

A city dweller was likely to be startled, even awed, at his first sight of a harrow in action. Comparing a time of trouble with ground subjected to the toothed implement, a painful experience was described as *harrowing*.

Sir Walter Scott used the earthy expression in his *Lady of the Lake*, thus making the term popular in standard speech.

HAVE SOMEONE'S NUMBER

Anytime you are sure you *have someone's number*, you are confident that you know a lot about that person. What is more, the information you hold probably isn't generally available.

In recent decades, the idea of possessing inside information as a result of having a person's number has been linked with our social security system. The IRS aside, you cannot function in modern American society without one of these nine-digit identifiers.

But in the early days of a telephone—before printed directories came into use—it was a person's telephone number that was all-important. In many communities, operators refused to ring unless a number was supplied. Since numbers weren't made available to the general public, anyone who had another's was possessed of almost magical access. Once that secret number responded, the ensuing conversation provided enough inside information for the caller to know the respondent in a special way.

HAVE THE GOODS ON

If you *have the goods on* a friend or family member, explanations are worthless; it is an airtight case.

That situation occurred with some frequency in decades after the Civil War. Counterfeiters flourished, taking advantage of paper money issued to finance the war. Beginners at the confidence game tended to keep bogus money on their persons. A fellow arrested with the green goods in his pocket didn't stand a chance when hauled into court.

Police came to speak of any damning evidence, not simply counterfeit bills, as *the goods*. When authorities *had the goods on* a suspect, their open-and-shut case was unlikely to be damaged by a high-powered defense lawyer.

HAYMAKER

When administered to a rival or competitor, a *haymaker* means that there won't be any more action any time soon. Though now linked with pugilism, the expression was originally rural.

A workman who exhibited skill and persistence with a scythe was termed a *haymaker*—because he made lots of grass ready to become hay. His repetitive motions produced the haymaker's jig, a folk dance in which his gestures were imitated.

Influence of the dance caused boxers to begin bragging about delivering blows as sudden as movements of a gyrating haymaker. Now the hoary term labels any blow good for a knockout—whether delivered in the ring or during a verbal bout around a conference table.

HAYWIRE

Moses P. Bliss launched a new era in agriculture and business when he patented a hay press in 1828. His power machine had many defects, but use of it was better than trying to tie loose bales of hay with string.

Demand for baled hay brought improvements that created bundles so firm they could be tied with wire. A major difficulty remained, however, as stiff hay wire easily became tangled or caught in machinery. At other times it would wind about legs of horses or snag clothing of workmen. When cut, wire sometimes snapped outward with enough force to cause an injury.

Until recent decades, production of hay in commercial quantities involved many accidents. As a result, we say that when a device or plan gets out of order, it goes *haywire*.

HELL ON WHEELS

Even though it involves no vehicle, some of us are likely to say that a really bad situation is *hell on wheels*. Tradition offers a logical explanation for this vivid expression.

Western lore has it that as soon as a transcontinental rail line was started, laborers and fortune hunters flocked westward. Just behind them were fellows determined to separate them from their fortunes.

Many long stretches didn't have a single outpost. That didn't stop canny operators from the East. They rented flatcars and used them to haul tiny brothels and mini-casinos. Pushed to the railhead, or halted anywhere else that potential customers could be found, one of these makeshift rigs figuratively constituted hell on wheels. Spreading slowly back to civilization, the vivid expression that seems all but meaningless proved just right to label any truly awful place or event.

Today the meaning has expanded and has become complimentary—used to label incredible skill as well as extremely rapid movement.

HENPECK

Biologist W. C. Allee gained fame by discovering the pecking order among hens. But a fowl's practice of using her beak as a weapon was noticed long before it came under the scrutiny of a scientist.

Aggressive wives were compared with fowls and said to *henpeck* their mates. Beginning late in the seventeenth century, writers began joking about male submissiveness. Even Lord Byron quipped that great ladies had "hen-peck'd" the nation's lords. Actually, henpecking of this type is limited to humans. Females of the barnyard peck one another with fervor, but let the lord of the barnyard alone.

Accurate or not, the metaphor is firmly established in speech. It is used to describe a female's verbal attacks upon a male—despite the fact that few, if any, roosters ever undergo henpecking.

HIGH GEAR

Anytime others notice that you are in *high gear*, you are sure to be going at a project or campaign at top speed.

Until auto gears became automatic, shifting of them took considerable attention and energy. Many sports cars now use the pattern: low gear, second gear, third gear, high gear, and reverse.

A vehicle equipped with four on the floor doesn't take to the road in high. Low gives power to start things rolling. Second offers an increase in speed, but reduces pulling power. When the vehicle moves into fourth gear it is ready for the maximum speed that horsepower and road conditions will permit.

All of which means that when you are in *high gear* you are moving very quickly and efficiently—that is, until you come upon a steep hill.

HIGH HORSE

When a friend's arrogance gets on your nerves, you may react with, "Get off your *high horse!*"

Long ago, a person's rank was fairly clearly indicated by the steed he or she rode. Donkeys were used by peasants and serfs, and run-of-the-mill horses transported shopkeepers and petty gentry.

Big stallions bred and trained as chargers for use in tournaments and in war were reserved for the rich and famous. Before Columbus made his first voyage to the New World, England's pageants usually included at least one rider mounted on such a charger, or *high horse*.

Today a person figuratively perched astride a big stallion is likely to be so pretentious that it calls for a rebuke.

HIGH ON THE HOG

Even if you are dining on seafood, when you are enjoying the best that is available you'll be said to eat *high on the hog*. That colorful expression doesn't have a complicated history.

When small farms dotted the countryside, every household raised a pig or two. No part of the animal was thrown away; even the intestines were savored as chitterlings.

Present-day purchasers of country-cured hams often saw off hocks and use them to season soup. Small slices that include whorls of fat can be cut from the lower part of the ham. But for a real feast, slices must come from *high on the hog*—above the center of the animal's leg.

HILL OF BEANS

Offered "a stand-out bargain" at a flea market, you may decline by silently or orally dismissing merchandise as being "not worth a *hill of beans.*"

These days, you would be hard put to find a literal *hill of beans*. In the era when many households grew their own food, everyone had plenty of them.

A cluster of seeds covered with a mound of earth constituted a hill. Long rows in the garden included so many hills that no one bothered to count them. For practical purposes this meant that a single hill of beans was so nearly worthless that its value couldn't be estimated.

HIP

If you are really up-to-date about what is going on, ready to deal with whatever comes, an admirer is likely to laud you as being *hep*. Not a bad characterization, really. For that's a shorthand way of saying that you are in step with the times.

Ordinary folk picked up the terse descriptive term from early jazz musicians. In the 1920s when jazz hadn't yet won a wide following, players often staged parades as a way of attracting attention to an upcoming performance.

Much in the fashion of a military drillmaster, the head honcho insisted that the musicians keep in step. Jazz being what it is, it was easy to effect a verbal transformation: "Step! Step! Step!" became "Hep! Hep! Hep!"

A player or a fan of the radical new form of music who was *hep* was literally in step with the marching band. Constant use led to development of an alternative form, so that a person who's "with it" may now be either *hep* or *hip*, usually the latter.

HOCUS-POCUS

If you've ever played around with rhyming words, you have company. This form of verbal recreation has been practiced for centuries in all cultures.

Early jugglers altered a Latin phrase used in the service of Holy Communion—a ritual in which ordinary bread is transformed. Magicians took the word *hocus* from classical terms for "Here is the body . . ."

Once that term had been coined for use in sleight-of-hand tricks, it was easy to form a rhyming partner. The result was *hocus-pocus*, which means you had better pay close attention or you will be badly fooled by what happens next.

HOGWASH

In Old England, male swine were often castrated so that their meat would remain tender and juicy. The castrated males were called *hogs*. This practice was followed by a ceremonial washing, after which the water was thrown out as worthless. This, according to oral tradition, gave rise to the expression *hogwash*.

That makes a good story, but *hogwash* involved neither castration nor cleansing. For generations this was the common name of swill fed to swine. Since the watery stuff might include no nourishment except table scraps and a little flour, it hardly rated as genuine food.

Exaggerated claims and tall tales are verbal *hogwash*, or talk that is not substantial.

HOLD A CANDLE

It was common in the sixteenth century and later for servants holding candles to guide their masters along the poorly lit streets of English cities. Theaters also employed candle-holders, called "link-boys," in the days before gas lighting.

Candle-holding was among the most menial of jobs, but some poor souls failed at them for not knowing the roads or the layout of a theater, and they were said to be not worthy to *hold a candle* to anyone. This expression soon came to be used in the sense of comparing abilities of two people.

HOODLUM

According to oral tradition, one of the most notorious ruffians of the Barbary Coast was known only as Muldoon. As the leader of a large gang, he commanded so much muscle that authorities were afraid to order his arrest.

During a clean-up campaign led by a San Francisco newspaper, a reporter had a great idea. Instead of referring directly to the underworld boss, he spelled the name backward as Noodlum. Then he changed the initial letter for *N* to *H*. Readers weren't long in figuring out who the mysterious Hoodlum was, and talk about his exploits propelled the made-up word into general speech.

That's the story still current in some parts of California, but wordsmiths believe it came from German immigrants. In German, the word *huddellump* means "wretch, miserable fellow" and thus "scoundrel."

HOOK, LINE, AND SINKER

During the colorful era when stories circulated largely by word of mouth, tall tales were popular and prized. Many fishermen tried to impress cronies by telling about a hungry one that didn't stop with the hook but gulped down the line and sinker as well. A tenderfoot from the East was likely to bite on almost any yarn. Compared with a ravenous fish, he was ridiculed as swallowing the tale *hook, line, and sinker*.

By the time civilization settled the frontier, the phrase had crossed the Atlantic from east to west. On both sides of the ocean, it is just right to label gullible and uncritical listening.

HOOKER

Tradition says that the name of hard-drinking Gen. Joseph Hooker of Civil War fame is behind the common label for a prostitute.

Orally transmitted stories have it that as military commander of Washington, D.C., Hooker encouraged prostitution "for the sake of the fighting men." Truth is, he never supervised the city's defenses. His longest hitch in D.C. was spent in what was once the insane asylum. When it was turned into a military hotel, he occupied a room briefly.

Another theory links today's label with the Corlear's Hook area of New York City. For many years, says tradition, this region was dotted with brothels patronized by sailors who referred to resident females as *hookers*.

Far less titillating, but much more plausible, is the theory that the hooker gained her name from one of the most innocent of sports: fishing. Until a prospective "John" takes the bait by looking, there is no need to waste time with him. Once his attention is hooked, there is a good chance that he will be added to a string of catches.

HORSE AROUND

More than any other large domestic animals, horses enjoy a vigorous frolic. Turned loose in a pasture, two or three or more of them are likely to run and jump as well as nuzzle one another. Such horseplay is spontaneous and seems to have little if any structure.

Every sizeable group of persons includes at least one who pays no attention to rules and precedents. Cracking jokes one minute and cutting capers the next, such a person likes to *horse around*—much like a stallion turned into a pasture with a couple of mares.

HORSEPLAY

During many centuries, horses were rare and expensive. Some knights actually did dash about Europe on spirited chargers. But oxen and donkeys were the most abundant and familiar beasts of burden.

The rarity of horses meant that it was quite an experience to see one of them frisking about a field or wallowing in dust. A big animal that lay on its back with all four feet flailing was obviously having a good time. So was a pasture mate who ran up to another in order to nuzzle.

Rough wallowing of a stallion and gentler romping of a mare was compared with boisterous action of humans. As a result, since the sixteenth century we have used *horseplay* to label rowdy and prankish behavior—indoors as well as outdoors.

HORSEPOWER

A steam engine invented by James Watt worked well but was criticized because there was no way to rate its power. Watt responded by measuring the pulling ability of a pair of big draft horses. One such animal, he calculated, could haul thirty-three thousand pounds one foot in one minute. So he named that unit of work the *horsepower*.

Soon afterward, in 1806, mechanical engineers said Watt had made a serious error. "Measurement of engines by horsepowers is wrong," they said, "because a typical horse can barely raise twenty thousand pounds one foot in one minute."

Debate continued for a century, during which the unit devised by Watt was called "shockingly unscientific." And yet engines powered by gasoline and electricity, as well as by steam, came to be universally rated in terms of their *horsepower* as measured by Watt.

From the Volkswagen to the Rolls-Royce, cars would be rated differently had Watt based his unit on the pulling power of ordinary nags instead of the heavy dray animals he actually used.

HORSE'S MOUTH

If you get a tip straight from the *horse's mouth*, you know that your informant considers it to be absolutely correct.

In spite of the fact that horses talk only in fables and television programs, the expression is worth using. As early as the sixteenth century, equine age was accurately estimated by examination of the mouth. Physical appearance and claims of the owners may be deceptive—but the lower jaw of a horse tells all to a person who knows the pattern of tooth aging.

When deciding whether or not to put money on a nag, a racetrack regular who gets a look at its teeth has accurate firsthand information about its age—secured straight from the horse's mouth.

The phrase *look a gift horse in the mouth* comes from this same practice. It was considered insulting to closely examine and inspect a horse that was a gift—as if you did not trust the donor to give quality.

HUMBLE PIE

Though we do not use the expression as frequently as in the past, it is not uncommon to hear someone refer to eating *humble pie.*

For centuries, dainty pies were made of umbles, or intestines of sheep. Just as chitterlings from intestines of swine are regarded as delicacies in many quarters today, umble pie was considered a mouth-watering confection in medieval England.

Differences in pronunciation led people to add an initial letter that transformed the meaning of the ancient term. Seldom available from the kitchen of a manor house these days, *humble pie* has come to be regarded as linked with humiliation rather than feasting.

HUNCH

Until the rise of scientific medicine, it was generally believed that a deformed person had special links with the demonic world. A gross malformation such as a hump or *hunch* in the spine was considered to be a mark of great psychic powers. Through his league with the devil, a hunchback was believed capable of seeing into the future. For centuries, accurate prediction was strongly linked with possession of a gnarled back. Consequently any premonition or flash of insight came to be known as a *hunch.*

HYPOCRITE

Western drama stems from that of the ancient Greeks whose term for actor was *hypokrites,* which was derived from the verb "to pretend." An actor pretended to be someone else. The word eventually came to mean a pretender or liar and, as such, passed through Latin and Old French into English.

In the fourteenth century, while creating the first English translation of the Bible, John Wycliffe had to indicate the idea in Matthew 23:10 of "playing the part of piety." He borrowed from the Greek and called the spiritual pretender a *hypocrite.* In spite of its earlier use in secular senses, the word was quickly linked with piety. Other shades of meaning disappeared, and *hypocrite* became the standard label for one who assumes virtue like an actor who hides his true self in a stage role.

IN THE DOGHOUSE

Couples who keep each other *in the doghouse* may not know it, but the expression goes back to the days of the African slave trade.

Profits in the evil business were great, but so was the danger. In addition to the hazards of crossing the Atlantic in sailing vessels, the slave trader was constantly menaced by the possibility that his "cargo" would break their chains and kill their captors. Therefore, many Yankee sailors slept on deck, after closing and locking the hatches at night.

Some sort of shelter was necessary, so many sailors covered the poop deck of the ship with tiny sleeping cubicles. Their small size suggested a doghouse. Though officers frequently had to sleep in them, they were so uncomfortable that *in the doghouse* came to indicate any state of discomfort—physical or mental.

IN THE GROOVE

Thomas Edison's first talking machine, made from a brass pipe into which spiral grooves had been cut, was a scientific marvel when it was patented in 1877. Tinfoil wrapped over the brass was indented by sound impressions and reproduced the sound with some fidelity. Everything went well as long as the clumsy needle remained in the groove. When the needle jumped from its place, pandemonium resulted.

A modified apparatus using a wax cylinder soon came on the market and was admired by all who heard it. But every operator was cautioned to keep the needle *in the groove,* and in time the phrase came to label any kind of good performance.

INDIAN GIVER

Because Columbus thought he had discovered a new passage to India, Native Americans came to be called *Indians*. Many were peaceful, but some were not. Women, bounty hunters, and many woodsmen were constantly alert to the danger of attack by Indians.

Frontiersmen coined dozens of phrases that included the name of their foes. Anything substandard, undesirable, or troublesome was called *Indian*. That is why a person who made a gift with conditions under which it could be reclaimed was ridiculed as an *Indian giver*.

In recent decades, admiration for whites who pillaged a continent and habitually broke treaties has diminished. At the same time, respect for the Native Americans has mounted. Yet a person who holds an option for reclaiming a gift is still called an *Indian giver*, albeit with a bit more discretion in these days of political correctness.

INSIDE TRACK

Anytime you're known to have the *inside track*, a rival or competitor will acknowledge that you have the best of it. At least in its earliest usage, the expression had nothing to do with hidden or inside information.

As might be expected, the phrase comes from the racetrack.

Most contests of any length were held on oval or round tracks. Contestants waited for the signal to begin while spaced out along the starting line. Everyone knew that the person having the slot closest to the middle of the course had a good chance of running a shorter distance than rivals.

In a footrace, the *inside track* was a major asset and logically came to mean a strong advantage in any situation.

IRONS IN THE FIRE

Modern householders who take the electric iron for granted do not always realize what a boon it actually is. Until electricity became available, it was necessary to heat an iron by placing it among the glowing embers of a fire or in the eye of a wood-burning stove.

The irons stayed hot only a short time, so it was customary to use several—ironing with one while the others were heating. It required no small amount of skill to keep the irons at the right temperature.

An amateur who tried to speed up work by using five or six flatirons usually discovered that it was difficult or impossible to keep up with all of them. If an iron remained on the heat too long, it became so hot that it scorched the garment on which it was used. A common tendency to have too many *irons in the fire* resulted in application of the expression to the broader sense of being involved simultaneously in too many activities.

JACKPOT

Rare, indeed, is the person who wouldn't like to hit a *jackpot* of one variety or another. To many a patron of casinos, the jackpot is much like a hole in one is to a golfer.

A big payoff as a result of hard work and ingenuity—or luck at a slot machine—owes its name to an intricate form of poker. In draw poker, a person must have a pair of jacks or better in order to open but has to ante regardless. If no one holds such cards, the pot grows larger and larger. Sooner or later, someone will rake in a pile of chips by hitting the *jackpot*.

JADED

English adventurers who first penetrated Iceland found it amazing. Nearly everything they saw added to their wonder—until they were shown a scrawny mare. At the sight of the puny native animal, they burst into laughter.

Travelers took home with them the Icelandic word for a mare and began to call any sorry, worn-out horse a *jade*. Some jades were foaled that way and couldn't help it. Others were once fine mounts that had been overworked and underfed.

In time, the Icelandic label transferred from a sorry mount to a weary rider. Even behind the wheel of a BMW, a person showing signs of exhaustion is compared with a hard-driven horse and described as *jaded*.

JAILBIRD

For centuries European law made some crimes punishable by public exhibition in a humiliating position. In England such offenses were usually the occasion for using the stocks. But on the Continent it was customary to place female prisoners in large iron cages suspended a few feet from the ground. Since the felon in such a predicament strongly resembled a bird in a cage, it became common to speak of her as a *jailbird*. The word caught the imagination of the public, and *jailbird* came to be applied to any criminal behind bars.

JAYWALKER

Few North American birds are as loud and colorful as the blue jay. Now often seen in towns and suburbs of cities, the noisy creatures once avoided humans. Their prevalence in wooded regions caused any rustic to be derided as a *jay*.

Male and female jays that ventured into urban regions often found themselves confused. Not understanding patterns of movement, and sometimes ignorant of signals, they seemed to endanger their lives when they tried to cross streets.

Sophisticated city folk jeered at any erratic pedestrian as a jay in action. Hence *jaywalker* became the standard title of a person who crosses a street in a reckless or illegal fashion.

JERRY-BUILT

A person shown a hastily constructed home or office is likely to reject it as *jerry-built*. That may be because the language of the sea remains alive and well in the speech of landlubbers.

Gales often snapped some of the masts of sailing vessels. Sailors responded by rigging temporary poles in order to try to make port. In their lingo, a flimsy upright likely to crash on the heads of crew members was often dubbed an *injury mast*. Abbreviated to *jury mast*, the name of the hastily erected timber seems to have been slurred to *jerry mast*.

Landsmen borrowed the expressive term and applied it to anything flimsy that was put together hastily. Like the old-time sailors' jury mast, *jerry-built* housing is likely to deteriorate almost before the newness has worn off it.

JINX

Back at the turn of the twentieth century, there was a resurgence of interest in the occult. Some persons who didn't have much faith in horoscope readings went all out for fortune-telling by use of animals and birds.

One of the most popular creatures for use in divination was the wryneck woodpecker—commonly known in much of the Southeast as the *jinx*. Many people who paid good money for information from a jinx regretted having tried to peer into the future. Too often, none of the predicted good came about—while all the bad omens proved to be true.

This denouement was frequent enough to give the poor little woodpecker a bad reputation; disaster followed a reading by means of a jinx so often that the bird's name came to stand for bad luck.

JOSH

Do you have to deal with a fellow worker or family member who's prone to *josh* around? If so, don't feel that you're alone—habitual jokesters and pranksters are found everywhere.

Such a person keeps us from forgetting about Henry Wheeler Shaw. That name doesn't ring a bell? Then try Josh Billings's byline, because *josh* was already in limited use to mean fooling around or kidding. Elevated into national prominence by one of America's most popular literary clowns, *josh* has found a permanent place in everyday speech.

JUBILEE

Though the word *jubilee* is loosely used to mean any occasion of great joy, it properly refers to any fiftieth-anniversary celebration. One of the most famous of these celebrations was the great Jubilee Year in honor of Queen Victoria's half-century reign.

The word goes back to an ancient custom of the Hebrews. They set aside each fiftieth year as a season of celebration and change. In that year, lands that had been sold were restored to their original owners or their heirs. Slaves were freed, and everybody took a rest. Not even the fields were cultivated.

The year was introduced by the blowing of a special trumpet in the temple. Such a trumpet was made of a ram's horn, or *jobel*, and the name became attached to the celebration. Passing through a number of languages, it entered English as *jubilee*.

JUMP THE GUN

Your circle of friends probably includes at least one person prone to *jump the gun* any time plans are beginning to be made.

Foot races and other events that test speed and stamina are often launched by means of gunfire. A contestant who is tense and uptight, straining every muscle in order to get a fast start, is likely to jump into action at almost any sound or movement.

But a racetrack with a pistol-wielding official isn't the only place where a premature start can be made. Almost any group activity, whether cooperative or competitive, can provide an opportunity for someone to *jump the gun*.

JURY

The legal processes of twelfth-century England were often informal. If someone seized a subject's property, the victim could buy a royal writ from the king to assure a hearing. The official presiding over the hearing would assemble a group of twelve neighbors who knew the facts of the case. Since the French-speaking Normans then ruled the island kingdom, the men who had to swear, or *jurer*, an oath to tell the truth came to be known as a *jury*. These "sworn" men reached a decision on the basis of personal knowledge related to the case. Lawyers later adopted the use of sworn citizens who relied on the evidence of others, and the modern jury came into being.

KANGAROO COURT

When the English explorer Captain James Cook returned from Australia in 1771, he was branded a liar. People disbelieved his reports of a strange animal that hopped about on two legs and stood as high as a man, which he reported the natives called "a kangaroo." Many who heard his accounts doubted their truth, and there was great joking about kangaroos.

When a few specimens were brought to Europe, they created a sensation. Anything marvelous or unusual was likely to be termed *kangaroo*. For example, an 1835 issue of the *Gentleman's Magazine* described an eccentric horseman as holding his reins with "kangaroo attitude." Settlers in the New World used the word to stand for any type of irregular gathering. During Reconstruction following the Civil War, a "kangaroo convention" held in Virginia made national headlines.

Criminals who adopted the odd word applied it to a "court" held by inmates of prisons. In such a proceeding, old-timers charged newcomers with such offenses as breaking into jail or being lousy and trying to scratch. Influenced by the prominence of irregular political gatherings, any extra-legal sham hearing came to be known as a *kangaroo court.*

KICK THE BUCKET

Until recent times, most slaughter of meat animals took place on the farm. Swine, sheep, and goats were comparatively easy to handle. Not so a steer that weighed a half ton or more.

A special hoist was devised for use with heavy animals. With its hind feet tied to a rope, a steer or an ox was pulled toward a beam at the top of a three-legged frame. A heavy wooden cask or bucket was shoved under the animal to prevent waste.

Frequently the rope was jerked as the puller strained to get a carcass into position. This action threw the feet of the animal against the bucket, almost as though it were deliberately kicking.

By the time a steer or a prize hog *kicked the bucket,* its throat had already been slit. Consequently the farm expression came into use to name death in any form.

KINGPIN

During the second century, Germans perfected a game in which wooden pins formed the target for a rolling ball. Arrangement of the target varied until the number of pins was standardized at nine—with a *king pin,* sometimes decorated with a crown, standing taller than the rest.

The Dutch brought ninepins to New Amsterdam circa 1600 and enjoyed it so much that authorities tried to suppress play. To get around the law, the size of pins was made uniform and a tenth one was added—and modern bowling was born.

Players no longer shot for a center pin tall enough to be regarded as regal. Yet the label of *kingpin* is still given to anyone standing tall enough to play a decisive role in a club, association, or board of directors.

KNOCK ON WOOD

It is a common practice to *knock on wood* with knuckles in order to try to ward off trouble or to seek good fortune. Almost invariably, this action of the hand is accompanied by a verbal announcement that it is taking place.

Ask a dozen acquaintances how this started, and at least one is likely to say that knocking turns a person's thoughts to the wooden cross on which Christ was crucified.

Knocking on wood as a form of asking for luck may just as easily stem from the play of children.

In many forms of the game of tag, trees afford sanctuary. A boy or girl who tags an oak or a pine is momentarily free from capture. But such knocking on wood doesn't count unless it is accompanied by a shout of triumph. That is, both actions and an announcement are required in order to assure the good luck that comes from safety.

KNOW THE ROPES

If you *know the ropes* at your place of work, you may be a candidate for the job of helping new employees to learn their way around.

Generations ago, ships' masters knew that a fellow fresh from land was little help at first. A full-rigged vessel had a seemingly insoluble tangle of ropes with which to set sails, and it took time and help to learn how to handle them. No man could hope to *know the ropes* until he had weathered the sun and salt spray for some time.

KNUCKLE DOWN

Facing a demand from the boss that you increase your productivity, you have two choices. You can put up a fight, or you can *knuckle down* to work like a veteran of the game of marbles.

Marbles are little round balls once made from the stone that gave them their name. Games played with them, popular for centuries, once came close to becoming the national pastime of England.

In many forms of play, each contestant is required to shoot from the exact spot at which his marble last stopped moving. That can't be done when a player's hand is upright, so it became standard to require that knuckles be against the ground before shooting. If a player seems tempted to move his marble, an opponent can demand that he *knuckle down*.

Spreading from marble rings of old, the expression gained currency as a way of describing earnest application to a task of any kind.

KOWTOW

Required to be obsequious toward a foreman or supervisor, some persons will walk off the job. Others will swallow their pride and *kowtow*. Anyone who follows the latter course imitates, after a fashion, actions that were standard in China.

Jesuits and other explorers long ago penetrated the mysterious East. Newcomers learned that in order to stay there, they'd better observe some Chinese customs. One of the most important was the ritual of *kotow* (later Westernized to *kowtow*). In it anyone brought into the presence of a person of higher rank knelt in formal fashion and touched his forehead to the floor or ground.

Physical kneeling never quite caught on in present-day American business, industry, family, or community life. But plenty of persons know what actions, words, and tones to use in performing a *kowtow*.

LAID-BACK

Most of your friends would say they were paying a compliment if they described you as being *laid-back*. In an era of tension it's a rare person, indeed, who deserves such a label.

It sounds as though it may have been inspired by envy of someone sprawled on a sofa, going nowhere and caring little. But in the world of language, logic seldom prevails. Couches and divans and beds did not give rise to the saying.

The design of many motorcycles is such that the rider seems almost to be reclining—a position quite unlike stiff and upright posture. Consequently, their laid-back posture came to symbolize a relaxed and easygoing manner in business as well as in pleasure.

LAY AN EGG

Did your favorite sports team ever *lay an egg*? Chances are that it did.

That expression sounds complimentary. When a barnyard fowl produces an egg, the critter is appreciated for its achievement. Not so in the human world, especially the realm of sports.

In the game of cricket, you scored a *duck's egg* if you had no runs at bat because an egg resembled the shape of a zero. What better way to express the notion of "no score" than to say a team laid a duck egg or a goose egg?

It is no longer necessary to make zero points in order to *lay an egg*. Any significant failure may evoke the expression that was once highly descriptive and self-explanatory.

LAZY SUSAN

In the antebellum South, some plantation owners were stern taskmasters. Others gave some servants, particularly those who worked in the kitchen, considerable latitude. One bright young woman, variously identified as having lived in Louisiana or in Alabama, decided to reduce the work of taking serving dishes from one person to another. She devised a variation of the rotating dumbwaiter usually used for wine. Since she had no surname, the circular rotating shelf she placed in the center of a dining table was jocularly called "our *lazy Susan*."

Though the yarn seems credible, it has no foundation. In use maybe a century ago, the name did not identify its inventor. Rather, it stood for any pert housemaid—or Susan—accustomed to working about the table of a rambling old homestead in Massachusetts or Connecticut.

LEAN OVER BACKWARD

As late as the eighteenth century, legal scales were weighted against accused persons. English judges of the period gained a reputation for an especially high-handed administration of justice. Many of these officials owed their appointments to political influence and were notorious for *leaning,* or showing open prejudice in favor of the prosecution. This was especially true in cases of treason because condemned traitors forfeited all their property to the crown.

Vigorous cleanup campaigns led to a period of careful appointments, and many new justices were alert to the civil rights of accused persons. To avoid any suggestion of leaning toward the crown, some of them went to opposite extremes. Such an overly conscientious judge was said to *lean over backward*, and the phrase came to stand for any stickler who went beyond the call of duty.

LEFT FIELD

Unless you felt led to take part in a crusade, it might be a good idea not to give an impression that you are out in *left field*. At least in modern conversation, this piece of turf is reserved for oddballs and wackos.

Such characterization was appropriate in days when the phrase referred to territory rather than attitudes. Once in a while, a topnotch ball player would wander or drift far into the left field. That meant he had little or no chance to catch any ball hit down a main alley.

Fellow athletes made fun of a player found out in left field two or three times a season. Fans learned to give such a fellow the Bronx cheer when he started to move. Originating on the baseball diamond, the derogatory term entered general speech to label any-one markedly unorthodox.

LEFT HOLDING THE BAG

Rural America of the nineteenth century had no fraternities or sororities, but hazing was a common ritual. Often it involved tak-ing an adolescent to hunt an imaginary bird, the snipe. Told that the snipe would dash into a heavy-duty bag that is properly held, the victim was made bag holder. Pranksters said they'd beat the bushes and drive the snipe into the bag—then slipped away, stifling their laughter.

When and where snipe hunting was invented, no one knows. But this rural method of poking fun at a gullible youngster was common. As a result, even in big cities where no one would wait for the imaginary snipe, a person who is tricked or swindled is said to be *left holding the bag*.

LEFT IN THE LURCH

Anytime you hopelessly outdistance a rival, he is likely to be described as having been *left in the lurch*. That's appropriate—for the expression was born in competition.

The French of the sixteenth century invented the game *lourche*, which came to be known as *lurch* in English. Few written records survive. Little is known about it except that large sums of money were frequently at stake in a game, which was somewhat like mod-ern backgammon.

Widely popular for a period, lurch was abandoned and nearly forgotten. But before its popularity waned, it became synonymous with competitive states in which one player is far behind. In crib-bage, for example, a state of lurch exists when one player has less than thirty-one points by the time a rival scores sixty-one.

Spreading from the gaming table, the expression survived long after the kind of play it names. Today a person *left in the lurch* is not in the running for an achievement, an honor, or a prize.

LEFT-HANDED COMPLIMENT

A reference to a *left-handed compliment* appears, on the surface, to refer to something laudatory said by a southpaw. But our everyday words and phrases often invite a look beneath the surface. In this case, such a peek takes us to medieval Germany.

Trying to discourage romances between noblemen and commoners, legal barriers were created. If a man of blue blood married beneath his class, a special ceremony was used for the wedding. In such a rite, the groom was required to give the bride his left hand rather than the customary right hand.

To a visitor from abroad, the special ceremony seemed quite ordinary. But a left-handed marriage hardly deserved the name. Neither the man's wife nor their children could gain his rank or property. This state of affairs led anything whose surface appearance was deceiving to be called *left-handed.*

After the sixteenth century, the left-handed wedding ceremony was seldom performed. But it made such a lasting impression that you get a *left-handed compliment* when offered an insult that masquerades as praise.

LET ONE'S HAIR DOWN

For decades, Paris has been the fashion center of the western world. Customs and sayings that originate there often become more firmly rooted in England and in America than in their native soil.

Noted entertainers and wives of wealthy nobleman have long vied with one another in creating new and elaborate hairstyles. It was once considered a serious breach of etiquette to appear in public without a coiffeur that required hours of work. Only in the intimacy of private quarters did beauties of the Napoleonic area relax by letting their hair down.

Moves toward pulling out pins and unbinding tresses came to be associated with relaxation. So any time inhibitions are discarded, we still say that a male or female *lets his or her hair down*.

LET THE CAT OUT OF THE BAG

British tenants who farmed land belonging to gentry were supposed to turn over part of all they produced as rent. Many adhered to the letter of the law, but some sold suckling pigs, considered a delicacy and easily carried, without reporting the transactions. Frequently concealed in bags while being taken to market, black market animals were bought by butchers at bargain prices.

By the eighteenth century, shrewd farmers had learned that in a hasty illegal sale, it was easy to pass off a cat as a young pig. When a suspicious buyer insisted on seeing the merchandise before he paid, he sometimes found his doubts confirmed.

Today, a person with inside information may slip and give clues. Even though neither a feline nor a bag is involved, comrades are likely to chide the revealer of the secret as having *let the cat out of the bag*. And a person who makes a hasty purchase without taking a look at merchandise is still said to have bought "a pig in a poke."

LIFE OF RILEY

Most people envy the lifestyles of the rich and famous. Stand-up comic Patrick Rooney exploited this feeling in a lilting song he wrote in the late 1880s.

Mr. Reilly, the central character of the Irish entertainer's song, didn't amount to much, but he was quite a daydreamer. Reilly imagined what he would do if he struck it rich in California.

Owning the railroads, he would not have to buy tickets. Having no need for money, he would turn down jobs that offered to pay "a hundred a day." Best of all, he would take over the White House and sleep in the president's chair.

Though Reilly existed only in the imagination of Rooney, he voiced the feelings of multitudes who paid little attention to the spelling of his name. Having heard or read lines that described the way Reilly conceived of life at the top, people began to wish they could step into the Irishman's shoes. Decades later, folks would still give their right arms for a shot at the *life of Riley*!

LIMELIGHT

Lighting was one of the chief problems of the early theater. In the time of Shakespeare, all available devices were crude and ineffective.

Actors, playwrights, and theatergoers were delighted when Thomas Drummond devised a new source of light in 1816. A cylinder of lime was heated to incandescence by a flame. When placed behind a lens or in front of a reflector, the *limelight* proved to be intensely bright.

The brightness made it ideal for use in making a star performer more visible. As long as one remained in it, audience attention was riveted.

Competition for a place in the *limelight* soon became intense. Consequently, it came to label any conspicuous spot—whether flooded by one of Thomas Drummond's lights or not.

LINGERIE

Good-quality cloth was costly as late as the Victorian era. Only natural fibers were used, so there was a definite limit to variety in weave and texture. French designers won international fame by creating distinctive garments from commonplace fabric. From ordinary linen (*linge*), they made exquisite linen dresses (*lingerie*) for special occasions.

Although women had more and more choices in outerdress fabrics, they continued to like the feel of soft *lingerie* next to their skin. Thus the name became attached only to intimate wear, even though it is now more likely to be produced from manmade fibers.

LION'S SHARE

When a bonus plan or vacation schedule is announced, it may not be equitable. Sometimes two or three people get the *lion's share* of the package.

In one of Aesop's fables, a lion, a goat, a sheep, and a heifer go hunting together. When a splendid deer is killed, the lion divides the venison into four equal portions. Then he seizes three for himself and suggests that his comrades may divide the fourth—if they dare.

Even when someone other than the boss of all the animals does the dividing, the one who gets the biggest portion automatically gets the *lion's share*.

LIVE WIRE

In the early days of household electricity, ordinary folks hardly knew anything about the newfangled way to control and use energy. Staring at a maze of wires, it was difficult or impossible for most people to fathom them.

Yet two things became common knowledge very early. Some wires carried no current and felt no different from anything else casually touched. But another wire in the same cluster would often yield a first-class jolt, or worse, when touched.

A wire of the latter kind was considered *live* because of the strong current in it. Some people are so full of energy that their blood seems to flow like an electrical current. Hence anyone who is always vibrant and ready to serve as the life of the party is known as a *live wire*.

LOADED FOR BEAR

If you ever face a situation of conflict in which you will be up against a tough and seasoned opponent, you had better be *loaded for bear*.

Why bear, rather than wolf or deer or moose? Because hunters of the frontier era found bears to be their toughest quarry. Nothing in nature is more dangerous than a full-grown bear wounded by a shot that failed to kill.

Tiny pellets packed into a shotgun were adequate for a squirrel or a rabbit. When a person went after a twelve-point buck, he loaded his gun with buckshot. And for the fiercest creature of the American wild, he stayed home unless he was *loaded for bear*.

LOCK HORNS

When you comment that a pair of antagonists *lock horns*, the expression may evoke an image of two angry steers going at one another head-to-head.

While such contests do take place in cattle pens, domestic animals did not give rise to the expression. It comes from the wilds of North America, where an old bull moose may boast antlers that weigh as much as sixty pounds.

Males are shy and unapproachable during most of the year but become aggressive as the autumn mating season approaches. Nature affords few spectacles more dramatic than that of a pair of giant swains with their spreading sets of horns locked in battle.

In frontier speech, angry humans were often compared with battling moose. As a result, we say that people who clash have *locked horns*.

LOCK, STOCK, AND BARREL

When you decide to put everything you have into an enterprise, associates are likely to comment that you're going for it *lock, stock, and barrel*. Anyone can take a half-hearted approach, but gumption is required for a decision to go all the way.

Muskets and rifles involved three major components: a carefully crafted lock, a stock made of wood, and a stout metal barrel. Each member of this trio was useless without the other two. Collectively, they came to indicate wholeness, completion, and, later, unhesitating and unreserved action.

LOOPHOLE

If you find a *loophole* in a contract or an insurance policy, it will constitute an escape route for one of the parties. This usage stems from a turnabout in understanding the name for what was once a special kind of tangible hole.

During the Middle Ages, architects and builders had to deal with the matter of defending a castle, once it was erected. Longbows, followed by crossbows, were formidable weapons typically used by both attackers and defenders. A narrow window, often oval at the top and wider at the inner side of a thick wall, was found to offer a difficult target from across a moat. At the same time, such an opening was big enough to enable defenders to fire at will.

This special form of *loophole* saved the hide of many lords of the manor. When firearms made it obsolete, its name transferred to any opening that provides an advantage to one party in a dispute or an agreement.

LOOSE CANNON

Any business or industry or neighborhood plagued with a *loose cannon* is a place in which to be constantly on the alert, as someone could get hurt.

Crewmen aboard an old-time man-of-war expected danger. They signed on knowing they'd probably be subjected to gunfire from enemy vessels. A broadside at two hundred yards was bad enough, but every veteran knew that the worst thing a sailor could face was a *loose cannon*.

Enemy fire, the pitching and tossing of a ship, and damage caused by hurling explosives sometimes caused the gigantic weapon to break loose from its mounting. Rolling and sliding around the deck, such a piece of naval artillery might smash anything or anyone it encountered.

That is often the case with a human who seems neither to know nor to care about holding a steady position. Rumbling and tossing through a force of workers or an organization, a two-legged *loose cannon* is a likely cause of major damage even when the ship of life is sailing in calm waters.

LUNATIC FRINGE

Expanding understanding of the human mind has led us to do away with long-established lunatic asylums. But the mind and its workings are far from being totally understood.

For countless generations, insanity was considered to be due to influence of the moon. Romans revered Luna as goddess of the sphere closest to earth, and credited her with enormous power. Her mood changes, reflected by what we know as phases of the moon, were believed to be responsible for many mental conditions.

Attributed to influence of Luna for many centuries, *lunacy* long labeled any significant aberration from what was considered to be normal. We now know that the moon seldom has anything to do with mental states. But since some persons who manage to function show signs of wobbling close to the edge, we continue to designate them as members of the *lunatic fringe*.

MACHO

A sampling of literature and newspaper clippings suggests that *macho* has been around since day one of our republic, but the now-universal label did not make its appearance until this century. Two factors appear to have combined to push it into prominence.

Increased presence of persons from Mexico, Cuba, and South America helped Anglos become acquainted with frequently used Spanish words—including the label for a fellow who is belligerent about his masculinity.

Flow of nationals into the United States accelerated about the time the feminist movement began capturing headlines. Anti-feminist protest, of a sort, was strengthened by adoption of the non-English title. Lots of men who were already *macho* but did not know what to call themselves now had a great new title, and thus it entered mainstream American speech.

MAKE A SCENE

Early playwrights had to take into account the physical limitations of small stages and the chore of shifting scenery by hand. As a result, they created divisions of fixed settings within an act, called *scenes.* Numerous entertainers gained fame for their performances in particular scenes. Such episodes usually invited a display of strong emotion.

Many theatergoers reenacted favorite scenes. Today we say a person who gives a theatrical display in everyday life is *making a scene.*

MAKE ENDS MEET

Full-rigged sailing vessels were equipped with a number of masts, each of which bore several sails. Since most pieces of canvas were raised and lowered separately, rigging involved hundreds of ropes. Many of these were movable, so they were easily repaired when they broke.

Some ropes attached to lower edges of sails were permanently fixed. When such a length of hemp broke, frugal masters ordered sailors to pull the ends together and splice them. In order to make both ends of a fixed rope meet, it was often necessary to strain and tug, stretching a piece of canvas to its limit.

Long used, literally, on the sea, we now apply the expression for succeeding with difficulty to anyone who *makes ends meet* by managing to stretch his or her income to cover all bills.

MAKE NO BONES

Elaborate menus were unknown to the common people of medieval Europe. Cooking vessels were rare and expensive, so vegetables were usually boiled in a single pot. Unless a housewife had a piece of meat large enough to roast, she usually tossed it in with her turnips, beans, cabbage, and carrots. Often a pot of stew included the neck, wings, and feet from a fowl or two.

Frequently a pot boiled for hours. Bones separated and became dispersed throughout the stew. This made it customary to eat with some degree of caution, removing the bones that were found. In addition to these real bones, fearful persons frequently gagged on imaginary ones. As a result, by 1450 a person making objections or showing hesitation of any sort was said to be *finding bones.*

This expression came into such wide use that people needed an equally forceful way of describing an opposite attitude. They found it by saying that those who plunge boldly into an undertaking *make no bones* about it.

MAKE THE GRADE

When you succeed in fund-raising or mastery of a new golf course, you *make the grade.*

U.S. railroads had only forty miles of track in 1830. Expanding from that base, engineers found that the pulling power of an iron horse is greatly affected by the slope, or *grade,* of a track. When a train moves from a level section to a 1 percent grade, five times as much steam is needed.

A grade of 3 percent or more challenged the power of locomotives and called for a celebration when the top was reached. Hence anyone who overcame obstacles of any kind was lauded by railroaders as having *made the grade*.

MARK TIME

When we say a person is forced to *mark time*, we use an expression that seems to be based upon watching a clock. In its earliest usages, it had nothing to do with timepieces of any kind. Instead, the term stems from activities of drill sergeants about two hundred years ago who demanded precision in movement.

One new exercise launched by the command *"Mark time!"* involved repeatedly lifting the feet without moving forward or backward, that is, marching in place. A solider engaged in this drill expended a lot of energy, but got nowhere. As a result, the sergeant's command came to designate any futile activity by soldiers or civilians.

MARSHMALLOW

One of the most common plants of medieval England was the mallow. It was abundant in many varieties; some hardy forms even grew among salt marshes. Long regarded as a weed, this *marsh mallow* suddenly burst into prominence when herb fanciers learned to make a potent medicine from its roots.

Syrup from the marsh mallow proved an effective remedy for coughs. Mothers experimented on their children and gradually came to regard the herb as a cure-all. According to a medical book published in 1680, the syrup was the sovereign remedy for half a hundred illnesses.

Someone later discovered that a novel confection resulted from mixing gum arabic with syrup of the marsh mallow. It proved so popular that a substitute was developed from gelatin and sugar.

Though not even remotely connected with herbs from England's marshes, the modern delicacy has taken over the name *marshmallow*.

MASTERPIECE

Trade guilds of past eras required an apprentice to learn by working under a veteran for nearly nothing, perhaps for years. The guilds stipulated that a person wishing to own his own shop had to be recognized as a master. After working for years as an apprentice, and later as a journeyman, a man could make a piece in his craft that would be considered that of a master's.

Once a man's *master piece* was approved, he was allowed to start his own business and hire an apprentice. For the rest of his life, he might look back upon his master piece as the finest example of his skill and ingenuity.

Passing from trade and industry of England to the fine arts, the term *masterpiece* came to label the finest individual piece of work or any product of an artist's most creative years.

MAUDLIN

Only slightly altered, the name of Mary Magdalene of biblical fame has become a household word. A favorite subject of medieval artists, Magdalene was almost always painted with eyes red and swollen from weeping. So anyone of similar appearance was spoken of as a *Magdalene*.

In common use the name was slurred over and capitalization was dropped. This produced the adjective *maudlin*, whose meaning gradually expanded to include the trait of effusive sentimentality.

MEXICAN STANDOFF

Nothing in the saga of Mexico matches the U.S. story of the gun-fight at the O.K. Corral. As depicted in countless movies and TV dramas, the Old West was a place where a cowpoke's gun was often his only friend. If shoot-outs had been as common as imagination makes them, the population of the whole region would have been wiped out.

Sometimes belligerents threw down on one another at the same split second. When that happened, they realized that both were about to go to Boot Hill. So they swapped insults instead of bullets.

In his prime, John Wayne would have preferred being dead to taking part in such a fracas. It reflected on a fellow's manhood to shove his gun into its holster and walk away from a standoff. Since everything and everyone from south of the border was considered inferior, the shoot-out that didn't happen was labeled a *Mexican standoff.*

Influence of cowboy lingo caused it to enter common speech to signify any stalemate between belligerents.

MIDDLE-OF-THE-ROAD

Until a generation after the Civil War, few great roads were built in America. Even those that linked major cities were likely to be narrow and poorly tended. Wheels of wagons and carriages kept the edges of many roads cut well below the level of the middle. That meant a person who walked along one in wet weather had to stay clear of the edges in order to keep feet dry.

Late in the century, cautious members of the Populist Party opposed union with Democrats. They wished to take a safe middle ground between extremes supported by political opponents. Someone mockingly referred to the cautious ones as *middle-of-the-roaders.*

This label stuck and continues to signify avoidance of extremes, long after the Populist Party died.

MILESTONE

Keenly interested in human development, observers of the modern scene tend to call any significant event or change a *milestone* of life.

Suggestive though it is, this usage is miles away from that of the Romans, who often went places and wanted to know how much distance was covered.

The Latin word for one thousand *(mille)* gave birth to the ancestor of the modern *mile*. Among the Caesars, this unit represented one thousand paces of five feet each. In order to make it easy to mark distances from the center of Rome, trained pacers placed stones along imperial roads at the end of every unit.

Scholars who translated classical documents reported systematic use of *milestones* at thousand-pace intervals. Adopted into English, the ancient term broadened to designate a turning point in a person's career or an important event in life.

MOLOTOV COCKTAIL

It used to be you couldn't follow the news for more than a few weeks without hearing of an incident of violence involving at least one *Molotov cocktail*. Gasoline-filled bottles with slow-burning wicks became staples in the arsenals of rebels and terrorists, who in more recent years have turned to even more deadly concoctions, contraptions, devices, and weapons.

Vyacheslav Mikhailovich Molotov had nothing to do with devising the crude but effective explosive. The Finnish named it after him because he was the premier of the U. S. S. R. at the time, and they were seeking freedom from the communist regime.

Freedom fighters who faced soldiers armed with heavy equipment and weapons adopted the use of gasoline-bombs in desperation. Derisively, they reported that they tossed such explosives in honor of the Soviet premier whose regime they resisted. Since a homemade device consisted of liquid in a bottle, it seemed right to combine the Russian's name with that of a drink and call it the *Molotov cocktail*.

MONKEY WRENCH

A friend or associate doesn't have to sport a long tail in order to throw a *monkey wrench* into plans and disrupt them. If monkeys used tools at all, a hammer would be easier to handle, so imagination long ago got busy trying to explain how their name attached to the tool.

One report has it that London craftsman Charles Moncke invented this special form of wrench and gave it his name. But even today, the British say "adjustable spanner" and not "monkey wrench." Another account would have you believe that the monkey wrench was developed by an American named Monk. No one has ever been able to find evidence that the tool was named for the first person to make it. A more probable explanation is that the people who first saw it may have laughed heartily. After all, a wrench whose lower jaw goes down or up at a twist of the fingers is about as ludicrous as a monkey jawing at onlookers in a zoo.

MONKEYSHINES

Until recent decades, exotic animals viewed by the public were always kept behind bars. Even the famous zoological gardens of England and Europe made little or no effort to put inmates into their natural habitats.

Monkeys, crowd-pleasers from the time they were first exhibited, are dexterous and smart. Like humans, they are quickly bored by monotony. So when a knot of admirers gathered before a cage squealing with delight and tossing peanuts, monkeys responded by putting on a good act.

Jumping, swinging about the cage, chattering and often seeming to grin broadly, little showmen knew how to work the audience. Bolder antics meant more peanuts.

Because a person believed to be trying to win friendship or admiration was said to *shine around,* antics of a monkey seeming to beg for acceptance were termed *monkeyshines.*

MORON

Almost everyone has been called a *moron* at least once. People who toss that label around usually do so without knowing that it is one of a handful of words formally voted into our language.

In 1910, a convention was held by the American Association for the Study of the Feeble-minded. Delegates complained that they didn't even have a name for persons with whom they worked. Someone reminded the crowd that a famous play by Molière had a dull-witted character named Moron who spent a lot of time center stage.

Maybe because the name is properly literary—and French, at that—workers with people we now label "handicapped" agreed to call every slow-witted individual a *moron.*

MOUSE

A wee rodent, usually brownish or grayish brown in color, abounds throughout the world. Its English name is derived from the same classical term that named the modern muscle—also small and often fast-moving. No known culture or civilization, ancient or modern, is known to have been without this creature.

Late in the twentieth century, engineers developed a little hand-held device used to control movements of a cursor on a computer screen. This device is small and rounded and has a cord that looks like a tail; hence, they called it a *mouse.* Although the shapes have changed some over the years, the catchy name is likely to remain.

MUCKETY-MUCK

Practically every organization, as well as every industry and business, has a high *muckety-muck*. Lots of citizens also know someone who holds that unofficial title in financial or social circles.

Traced to its roots, this earthy phrase means simply, "a person who has plenty to eat."

It appears to have sprung from European attempts to understand the jargon of Native American tribesmen. In periods of scarcity, only chieftains and their families had enough *muck-a-muck*, or native food.

Trying to imitate a vivid pattern of sounds, settlers seem to have garbled it. So the notion arose that a person becomes a high *muckety-muck* through importance—rather than through having a full belly when others are hungry.

NAG

Folk tales from the Middle Ages reveal that rats were prevalent in many towns and cities. They not only ate food that humans needed, their gnawing was a constant source of irritation. Householders could do little to get rid of rodents, so they simply had to endure their noise.

An old Scandinavian term for the process of gnawing passed through German to English—and emerged as *nag*. Eventually it was applied to any persistent irritation, not simply the biting on wood and nuts of rats and squirrels. Contrary to logic, therefore, the word has nothing to do with the activities of a worn-out horse.

A common source of annoyance, then and now, centers in persistent scolding by a member of the family, a fellow worker, or friend. Hence, we still say a person who gnaws at another by constant fault-finding is nothing but a *nag*.

NARROW-MINDED

Though he never held the title, Ben Jonson is widely considered to have been England's first poet laureate. After producing a smash hit in 1598, he became the chief literary lion of his era.

His last great work, *The Staple of the News*, was finished in 1625. By then, anything he wrote was sure to be widely read and quoted. So when he used a vivid title for a prejudiced person, it became popular in language. Writing of a man whose "thoughts be dwell All in a Lane," Jonson described him as being "narrow-minded."

Launched in this fashion, the expression was quickly adopted by sophisticates of the era. Many used Jonson's term jokingly at first, but it proved so expressive that we still turn to it when we wish to label a person as having a restricted outlook or as being provincial.

NEGLIGEE

French society reached heights of extravagance and ostentation under Louis XIV. Ladies were expected to spend hours dressing themselves before any formal occasion. Sometimes this pomp and ceremony lost its zest. Many a beauty dressed casually in the privacy of her own room at the cost of being criticized for her *négligé* (neglected) attire.

Designers eventually created loose, comfortable dresses for periods of relaxation. Naturally they took the name by which informal clothing was already designated. In this form the *negligee* was popular for more than a century and was associated in popular thought with uninhibited conduct in rather intimate surroundings. Gradually *negligee* took on the more limited meaning of a loose dressing gown.

NIP AND TUCK

Many common words and phrases were brought westward across the Atlantic Ocean from England. Once the Colonies were flourishing, the stream of language began to flow eastward to the mother country. That was the case with an expression now linked with a neck-and-neck finish of a contest of any sort.

Since cloth was scarce and expensive, Colonial tailors followed their patterns very closely. This skimpiness could pose problems when a segment was being fitted into a garment.

Skilled workers learned how to nip a problem piece here and there with scissors, then tuck it into place. This procedure might produce a tight fit, but it saved a lot of cloth, and cloth was money.

Originating in the speech of Colonial tailors, *nip and tuck* was borrowed by the English—who, like us, use it to describe a contest so close as to leave the outcome in doubt. More recently, the phrase has become common parlance among those with a fondness for plastic surgery, but that's a whole 'nother story.

NIP IN THE BUD

Crude beginnings in scientific horticulture were made many centuries ago. At least as early as the fourteenth century, gardeners knew that many plants produced an excessive number of blossoms. So it became customary to pinch off the majority in order that those which were left might produce large fruit.

This practice improved the quality of garden produce—but was devastating to individual buds. It became proverbial that when a bud was nipped off, no fruit would be produced at that point. Comparing the gardening practice with human activities, a person who calls an early halt to a plan or enterprise is said to *nip it in the bud*.

NITPICKER

Many groups of people include a *nitpicker*, prone to concentrate upon insignificant matters and complain about them. Bellyaching about trifles might be reduced or stopped if such a person knew the source of his or her title.

Middle English, a language almost as distinctly different from Old English as from modern English, modified an old term and called the egg of any parasitic insect a *nite*. With the final letter omitted in contemporary usage, the word is most often employed to label an egg of a body louse.

Such an egg is so minute it is too small to be seen except with keen eyes. But because of its shape and texture, it is fairly easily discovered by probing with the fingertips. Frontiersmen who didn't like to be lousy learned to find nits and pick them off the skin so they wouldn't produce insects. Many caged monkeys, incidentally, exhibit great skill in this activity.

A person or a monkey busy trying to find and remove the tiny eggs doesn't have time or energy for big and important things. As a result, anyone who concentrates upon discovery of very small errors and faults is disparaged as a *nitpicker*.

NO SPRING CHICKEN

Archaeologists have found evidence that humans began keeping poultry at the dawn of civilization. Already ancient in the time of Julius Caesar, this type of husbandry spread throughout the world. Until recent generations, there were no incubators and few warm hen houses. That meant chicks couldn't be raised during winter.

New England growers found that those born in the spring brought premium prices in the summer market places. Sometimes they tried to deceive customers by offering old birds as though they belonged to the spring crop.

Wise buyers would protest that a tough fowl was *no spring chicken*. As a result, the barnyard term came to designate persons, as well as birds, past the plump and tender age.

OFF THE DEEP END

Friends are likely to say that a person ready to take an unnecessary risk is about to go *off the deep end*. Sometimes the same expression is applied to one in danger of flipping his or her lid or overreacting.

Indoor swimming pools proliferated about the time of World War I. In many YMCAs or other recreational buildings, there were no lines showing the depth of the water. Swimmers familiar with the place knew which end was deep, while newcomers who hit the water at its deepest point were sometimes in trouble.

It was these swimmers—rash to take on more than they could handle—who inspired the expression.

OFF THE WALL

Why do we sometimes say that a really unusual piece of artwork or a ridiculous plan is *off the wall*? Because a wall is essential to several popular games, notably squash and handball. In them, as well as in racquetball, a bounce from the wall is influenced by speed, spin, and angle. Even a veteran player cannot always estimate what direction a ball will take.

Like a ball bouncing at a weird angle, a plan or an activity may be so unpredictable that it, too, is described as being *off the wall*.

OK

When you're carefully scrutinized and pronounced to be *OK*, you know you'll get an insurance policy, a promotion, or an extension of your credit. Anytime that happens, you can thank an often-overlooked president of the United States.

Admirers of Martin Van Buren, born at Kinderhook, New York, lauded him as Old Kinderhook when at age fifty-eight he made a bid for a second term in the White House. Running against war hero William Henry Harrison, it was to be an uphill battle.

Democrats of New York City formed a booster club and launched a campaign to raise money and win votes. On March 23, 1840, the city's *New Era* newspaper published an announcement: "The Democratic O.K. Club are hereby ordered to meet at the house of Jacob Colvin on Tuesday evening."

During a heated campaign that fizzled in the end, the president's abbreviated nickname popularized the rare New England phrase. Since then, the American-born political slogan has spread around the world.

OLIVE BRANCH

Egyptians began experimenting with a native shrub at least four thousand years ago. Soon they produced varieties that yielded fine oil. As a result, the olive came into cultivation around the entire Mediterranean basin.

In the biblical story of the great deluge, a freshly plucked olive branch was the first thing to give hope to Noah and his shipmates. Soon this harbinger of good tidings was followed by a promise that the flood would never be repeated.

As a result of that memorable incident, an *olive branch* became a symbol of peace and goodwill. Even in lands far too cold for the evergreen tree with edible fruit, the expression born in Egypt is almost universally understood.

ON A ROLL

Anytime you're congratulated as being *on a roll*, you are seen as unbeatable for the moment. Such a winning streak, regardless of the field of activity involved, takes its name from gaming tables.

Every crapshooter, beginner or veteran, yearns for the time when each roll of the dice will produce another in a long string of wins. A first throw of seven or eleven signals that this may be the instant at which luck will start.

Lots of persons have either experienced this work of chance or watched others profit from it. Consequently, anyone enjoying a great streak of luck is lauded as being *on a roll*—even when a pair of dice is not involved.

ON THE BALL

When you win an honor or achieve success against odds, chances are good that someone will say you have something *on the ball*.

This term of commendation was coined by early fans of baseball. Though it has much in common with rounders, long played in England, baseball elevates the pitcher to special prominence.

Pioneer hurlers discovered that they could deceive unwary batters by spinning the ball so that it didn't travel in a straight line. Their prowess caused the diamond-born expression to be used as a term of admiration for skill and proficiency displayed anywhere and any time.

ON THE BEAM

It's logical and natural for colleagues who see that you are headed straight toward a solution of a problem to say they're glad you are *on the beam*.

Our earliest aviators had no guidance systems, and airports were not equipped to send radio beams into the air. Wilbur and Orville Wright and other pioneers flew strictly by the seat of their pants.

Introduction of guidance beams from the ground with receiving sets on planes worked a miraculous transformation. By using them, a pilot could locate a beam and use instruments in order to follow it to a base.

Small wonder that a person or a plan or an enterprise not wavering from an objective is lauded as being *on the beam*.

ON/OFF THE CUFF

Electronic transmission of information now makes it difficult for anyone to treat debts casually. If a person has an outstanding obligation, a quick search is likely to reveal it. Today's transactions are a far cry from what they were a few generations ago.

So is easy credit. As late as the era of Theodore Roosevelt, many merchants seldom let people get merchandise without putting cash on the barrel head. Credit was so limited that a fellow operating a livery stable could keep his records on his shirt cuff.

Which meant that a drifter who lived *on the cuff* was adept at talking folk into extending credit without formality. Casual business transactions were common enough to cause anything impromptu to be termed *off the cuff.*

ON THE HOUSE

Anything distributed free of charge, courtesy of the management, is said to be *on the house.*

Originally, the house involved was an English pub or tavern. Owners often invited newcomers to sample their stock by offering a free drink. This small taste often whetted the appetite for more, and the barkeep could expect the sale of several more drinks.

Some U.S. states prohibit a barkeeper from offering freebies; in other regions, rising costs have made the custom obsolete. Despite this, we say that gifts to a consumer from a business owner are *on the house.*

ON THE SKIDS

Until modern machines were developed, movement of goods for even short distances could be a major chore. To save time and cut down on labor, Americans constructed ramps and platforms made of heavy timber, or *skids.* Often slanted sharply, these devices were ideal for rolling logs or barrels. With practice, it was easy to slide many other things down such an inclined framework—especially if it was greased.

Once a barrel or a bale was placed in position and given a push, it was on the skids and headed downward out of control. This strongly suggests that when a person's career or character is seen by others to be *on the skids*, then he or she is headed for a downfall.

ON THE SPOT

Police courts of the past and present have often disregarded the legal rights of prisoners. Officers in charge of such courts have sometimes used every possible means to secure a confession from a suspect. Open brutality prevailed until the latter part of the nineteenth century when aroused public opinion led violent methods of "questioning" to become illegal.

As a substitute for violence, mental and physical ordeals were devised. One of these methods consisted of forcing a suspect to stand *on the spot*—a tiny square marked with chalk. Without permitting a prisoner to move from the spot, officers would bombard him with accusations for hours. While forced to remain on the spot, it was dangerous to say anything, yet the accused couldn't ignore all of the questions fired at him. Borrowed from police jargon, the phrase came to name the state of being in any delicate or dangerous position.

OPEN AND SHUT

Few card games have had a more hectic reign than faro. Sweeping to popularity about 1850, it became a major means by which prospectors were separated from their gold dust.

Standard play of the era included numerous complicated ways to place or raise bets. Novices were discouraged by these technicalities, so a gambling hall operator devised a simpler version. In this modified faro, the pot was shut very soon after having been opened.

Veterans of the pasteboards preferred the older and more challenging game and so turned up their noses at *open and shut* play. Spreading from gold fields into general speech, the expression from the faro table came to name any uncomplicated situation.

ORDEAL

When you undergo an *ordeal* at work or on a shopping expedition, you've had an exhausting and probably painful time. Pain was the essential element in medieval rituals that concerned the judging of others.

In the eras before accused Englishmen were brought before judges and juries, innocence was frequently determined by an *ordeal*. Authorities sometimes heated a bar of iron and offered it to a person suspected of crime. If grasped without burning the flesh, their deity was considered to have rendered a verdict of innocent. Numerous other ordeals were used with accused person; in all of them a person was pronounced guilty if he or she showed signs of suffering.

Expanding from kangaroo courts into everyday life, the name of a physical test came to indicate a relatively low-level experience that is only trying or vexatious.

ORIENTATION

Orientation week has become a familiar institution on the college campus. Many industries have adopted a similar period of "breaking in" new employees. Though such formal practice of orientation is modern in origin, it represents the latest in a long chain of developments.

During the Crusades in which Christian Europe tried to recapture the Holy Land from its Moslem conquerors, religious zeal made east the key direction. From an ancient term for "direction of the sun's rising" the East was known as *the Orient*. Medieval cathedrals were built with their long axis due east-west with the chief chancel or altar at the orient or eastern end. Pious folks frequently insisted on being buried with their feet pointing east. As late as 1775, mapmakers marked the east with a cross.

From the process of pointing to the Orient, or getting one's bearings, *orientation* came to signify all types of alignment, whether toward the geographical Orient or some other direction in ideas or space.

OUT OF LINE

Anytime you notice someone who is noticeably different from colleagues in actions or ideas, that person may be badly *out of line* without knowing it.

At least two areas of activity could have spawned the expression.

A military line is not only expected to be as straight as an arrow; each person in that line should move simultaneously. Coordinated movement is even more important in a chorus line; a single kicker who is a split-second off can make the entire line look ragged.

However the term entered the language, in today's usage a person with generally unacceptable ideas or behavior may be disparaged for being *out of line*.

OUT OF TOUCH

Late in the eighteenth century, many European military leaders moved toward use of tighter formations. Men were required to maintain rigid patterns even when on the march. As a practical way or regulating his space, the soldier in the ranks had to be sure that his swinging elbows would touch those of comrades on each side.

Whenever there was a gap in a line, it meant that some man was literally *out of touch*. Civilians adopted the military term and expanded its meaning to indicate any situation in which a person has lost contact.

OUT ON A LIMB

A person who finds himself or herself *out on a limb* is in a precarious position, with no sure or easy way to get out of the predicament.

That is precisely the situation of a possum or raccoon that takes to a tree and misjudges the distance to another. Having moved far out on a limb in order to jump to safety, such an animal suddenly realizes that there is no escape from its pursuer. It is too far to jump, and dogs are already under the tree, barking to bring hunters for the kill.

Though barely a century old in literary use, the hunting term born on the American frontier may have been used orally as early as Colonial times.

OUTLANDISH

Nearly every body of speech reflects suspicion of foreigners, or casts aspersions on them. That was the case with Anglo-Saxon English, which brought the Dutch word *uitlander* to British soil. By the 1600s, this word became *outlander*.

Costumes and customs from other lands can seem odd. As a result, any comment concerning an outlander was likely to produce a laugh. Henry Fielding took advantage of this when he wrote the famous novel *Tom Jones*. In it, he jeered at a young woman whose clothing he described as being "outlandish."

This and other literary appearances gave respectability to the earthy old peasants' term. Unchanged in spelling since the seventeenth century, *outlandish* is now applied to anything bizarre or uncouth—whether it is of foreign or native origin.

OUTSKIRTS

Radical changes in every area of English life resulted from the conquest of the island by William the Conqueror. Norman ladies turned up their noses at simple Anglo-Saxon clothing and wore an elaborate outer garment, which they called a *skirt*.

Soon it was observed that a fringe of houses clustered outside town walls was much like a skirt surrounding a woman's feet. So it became customary to speak of a city's edge as its *skirts*. Naturally, one who wished to indicate a house or inn lying at the extreme outer border of a community described it as being in the *outskirts*.

OVER A BARREL

Unless you have suddenly found yourself *over a barrel*, you can hardly imagine how dreadful such a situation can be. Financial reverses, a failed love affair, and pressures on the job are only a few of many things that can make a person feel absolutely helpless.

That is precisely how mobs of yesteryear wanted some of their targets to feel. A person considered too guilty to escape with tar and feathers was often publicly whipped. To prevent wriggling while the lash was being applied, a victim was tied to an overturned barrel. Though the feet remained firmly on the ground, the upper body was bent to follow the curve of the barrel.

Today, anyone figuratively bent *over a barrel* while waiting for the worst to come is in a dreadful fix with little or no hope of escape.

OVER THE COALS

If you threaten to haul someone *over the coals*, the object of your suspicion or wrath is in for real trouble.

A tongue-lashing is nothing compared to fearful ordeals faced by accused persons for many centuries. In the belief that God protects the innocent but permits the guilty to suffer, a trial often consisted of a physical test.

Frequently a suspect was forced to walk barefoot over a bed of hot coals. Burns brought an automatic verdict of guilty. But anyone who passed the heat test without injury was judged to be innocent. Onlookers at such a trial remembered it so vividly that its name attached to a severe test even if fire was not involved.

PAINT THE TOWN RED

Many a celebrating individual has set out to *paint the town red*. So have lots of visiting conventioneers who would like to turn a convention into a spree.

Why this color, always, instead of, say, a green or blue foray once in a while? One theory links red with the flames of pioneer villages set afire by marauding Indians. Somehow, it seems inappropriate to compare the notion of a high-rolling good time with watching a cluster of houses burn to the ground.

A more plausible explanation suggests that fast action in red-light districts, or streets crowded with brothels, contributed to development of the phrase.

Red is the color of excitement in so many cultures that they cannot be counted. So it is at least an even chance that the American who first spoke of *painting the town red* simply chose that expression as a way to express the notion of having a really exciting time.

PANDEMONIUM

Next time you find *pandemonium* breaking out around you, maybe you can shut out some of the noise by thinking of John Milton.

Why Milton, rather than some other immortal poet, novelist, or playwright? Because he's the indisputable father of the label we apply to a chaotic uproar. Only a handful of persons have managed to coin a new word that has lasted. Milton was one of the few.

Writing of "the high Capital of Satan and his Peers" in his famous *Paradise Lost*, Milton combined the Greek words *pan* for "all" and *daimon* for "demon" into *Pandaemonium*—meaning literally "the place of all demons." His readers modified the spelling into today's more familiar form. Only a rare master of words could have thought of combining these five syllables in such rhythmic and evocative fashion.

PANIC BUTTON

Should circumstances ever cause you to hit the *panic button*, that would be a signal for others to act quickly in order to forestall disaster.

The original panic button could be found on a U.S. bombing plane—a B-24 or a B-17. When that button was pushed by the pilot, it activated a bell that functioned even when the intercom system was shot full of holes.

Numerous crew members were at a distance from the cockpit, unable to know when flak damage called for ditching the plane. At the first signal from the panic button, they dropped what they were doing and prepared to make a hasty exit. A second signal constituted an imperative command: "Jump! Jump now!"

Transferred to civilian life, the airman's signal for quick action to avert catastrophe led us to say that a person who issues an imperative warning—orally or in writing—has hit the *panic button*.

PARAPHERNALIA

Until modern times—and still in some parts of the world—a bride's family had to provide her husband with a dowry. Such a marriage settlement became the personal property of the man. He could dispose of it as he pleased, and even at his death his wife could not claim it. The wife owned absolutely nothing.

Under Roman law, however, a woman's personal property other than the dowry remained under her control. Her husband could exercise no rights over it, and when he died, it was not included in his estate.

Such property was called *parapherna*, from the Latin word for "beside dowry." Women's rights in *parapherna* were included in most western European codes, which were based on Roman law.

Though there were exceptions, such belongings usually consisted of jewelry, furniture, clothing, and odds and ends. As a result, the word came to stand for any miscellaneous collection of furnishings. Legislation concerning property rights of women made the term obsolete in its legal sense, so *paraphernalia* now stands for any group of articles a man or woman might accumulate.

PASS THE BUCK

A person who is inclined to *pass the buck* when pressed isn't likely to move up the corporate ladder very fast.

Neither is the buck passer the most likely candidate for winning a card game. For the buck used in such a game is a token, formerly a piece of buckshot that indicated the position of the deal. In several kinds of play, the dealer has special responsibility. His opening wager will determine whether the pot is likely to be large or small.

A cautious fellow who wishes to avoid taking the initial plunge hesitates when the buck reaches him. At many tables, he's given the privilege of passing the buck so that the next player becomes the dealer.

Inevitably, anyone who evades making decisions or accepting responsibility of any sort is said to *pass the buck*. Very early in the life of the phrase, it became closely attached to politicians and office holders.

PAY THE PIPER

Street dancing was a chief form of amusement during medieval times. However, not every flute player could pipe for a dance, so there developed a class of strolling musicians who would play for a dance wherever they could gather a crowd.

Frequently a dance was organized on the spur of the moment. Persons who heard the notes of a piper would drop their work and join in the fun. When they tired of the frolic, they would pass the hat and take up a collection for the musician. It became proverbial that a dancer had better have his fun while he could; sooner or later he would have to *pay the piper*.

PAY THROUGH THE NOSE

Anyone caught in a squeeze that cannot be escaped without meeting an exorbitant demand will have to *pay through the nose*. This unpleasant course of action, according to legend, stems from the brutality of warriors who overran Ireland long ago.

According to the story, Norsemen who mastered the land about a thousand years ago demanded heavy tribute. Anyone who couldn't, or wouldn't, pay was seized and suffered a slit nose. Those who escaped this brutal punishment told their descendants that, once upon a time, they were forced to *pay through the nose*.

It makes a great tale—Ireland really did fall to Norse invaders in the ninth century. But there is no record that conquerors offered the option described. Eight hundred years passed before a literary work included a character who was forced to pay through the nose.

Common sense, not backed by proof, suggests a much later and more commonplace origin. When a quarrel erupted over money and one party ended with a bloody nose, the victor surely could have crowed that the loser was made to *pay through the nose*.

PECKING ORDER

Observation of the *pecking order* within your circle of friends or fellow workers will tell you who is really boss and who's actually on the bottom.

Biologist W. C. Allee gained fame from the study of hens. Every barnyard flock, he found, has a clear pattern of social prestige. Any hen pecks freely at those below her rank but submits meekly to the pecking of those above her.

Male-female pecking occurs among humans, but in a flock of chickens no hen pecks a rooster. That means the barnyard term—apt and vivid as it is—is strained somewhat when applied to people.

PETER OUT

Peter Schmidt, says oral tradition, wandered into the Ohio River Valley as a day laborer. He talked a good game and found it easy to get a job. For a day or two, maybe even a week, he would work hard from sunup to sundown. Then his pace would slow down and he would begin cutting his hours. Before the end of the month, he would *Peter out* and be fired.

Explanations like this one, called "folk etymology" by scholars, don't stand up under scrutiny. Instead of being named after a man who burned hot and then rapidly cooled, miners coined the phrase we use to mean "dwindling to an end."

Forty-niners used a mixture of charcoal and saltpeter—the active ingredients—to make explosive charges. With its name clipped to *peter*, the stuff made short work of stones. But liberal use of peter could exhaust a seam quickly.

A mine seen to be yielding less and less dust was recognized by veterans as about to *peter out*. Fixed in speech during the gold rush, the effect of using explosives is applied to any business or enterprise that is obviously dwindling.

PETTICOAT

It was normal in the Middle Ages for a man to wear a petticoat. When knights wore armor, their bodies needed protection against chafing at the shoulders and the unpleasantness of very cold or hot metal.

Therefore, an ingenious tailor conceived the idea of making a short, snug, padded coat to wear under the coat of mail. Because such a garment was smaller than the ordinary coat, it was termed a *petty-coat*. Soldiers were loud in their praise of the petty-coat. Civilian men began to wear them under their doublets and women under their dresses. Over a period of centuries the word *petticoat* became restricted to a woman's underskirt.

PHONY

When you say that a piece of jewelry or a work of art is *phony,* you owe the label to early Irish sharpers. One of the favorite ruses of those con men became known in England as the *fawney rig.* The original Irish word for a finger ring was *fáinne;* Englishmen familiar with the trick changed the word to *fawney.*

A con artist using this stratagem put a ring, or *fawney,* in a public place. Sooner or later someone would come along and pick up the piece equipped with an imitation stone. Appearing from nowhere, the swindler persuaded or frightened his victim into paying him to keep quiet about the find. Making off with hush money, the sharper would leave the sucker holding a fawney that seemed valuable but was actually worthless.

So many persons were defrauded that anything fake came to be called *fawney.* The word was finally Americanized to *phony.*

PICAYUNE

Spanish adventurers who settled in Florida and Louisiana established their own currency system. Its smallest unit was the half real, worth about six and a quarter cents and known to later Creoles as the *picayune.*

Merchants and traders didn't like to deal with picayunes because many customers were prone to quibble over its exact value in merchandise. This annoyance led the name of the coin to be attached to anything of trifling value. Consequently a person who quibbles or finds fault over any petty matter is said to be *picayunish*, or as troublesome as a frugal housewife spending a picayune.

PIG IN A POKE

Never buy a *pig in a poke*; always take a look at merchandise before handing over payment, regardless of how great a bargain is offered.

That advice wasn't always heeded in early England, so many purchasers were stung by shrewd farmers. Until three months or so old, a young porker usually went to market in a heavy bag, or *poke*, that was carried over the seller's shoulder by means of a stick.

More frequently than we'd like to think, in "the good old days" a farmer's poke held a sick or deformed piglet, and sometimes even a cat, that was offered at a price below the market. If a prospective purchaser asked to take a look, the seller was likely to refuse to open his bag "because once little pigs get loose, they're almost impossible to catch."

Lots of folk who had a taste for pork and took a stranger's word actually bought a pig in a poke. Too often, a quick look inside the bag revealed that what seemed to be a good buy was money wasted.

PIGEONHOLE

Attitudes toward many things we use daily go through cycles. There is a period of excitement when something new is put on the market; then a replacement comes into vogue. As years pass, articles in attics and basements are seen as antique and valuable. That is when replicas come out.

Desks used by merchants and teachers and others have gone through every phase of this cycle. When it first became available, a piece with rows of rectangular compartments was an eye-catcher. Its little segments looked like holes in a pigeon roost, or *côte*. So a piece fitted with them was called a *pigeon-hole desk*.

Used for decades, then mostly discarded, replicas of the desk are now available. Of course, a good one will cost you a lot more than an original when it was new!

So many people sorted letters and bills and invoices and reports into *pigeonholes* for so many years that the noun was made into a verb of action. We use it to name any process of classification or as a symbol of putting something into a narrow slot.

PIGGY BANK

A fifteenth-century pot or jar made from one kind of clay was called a *pygg*, from an obscure word for the clay. Evidently this raw material was abundant, for its name eventually attached to all earthenware.

Then as now, frugal housewives frequently dropped their coins into a pygg for safekeeping. Perhaps influenced by the old name of the earthenware container, potters of the 1800s began making pig-shaped coin holders for children. This practice caught the public fancy so effectively that it became customary to call a coin box a *piggy bank*, no matter what its shape or composition.

PINCH HITTER

Every club and organization, along with practically all business enterprises, sometimes gets in a tight spot. Action is needed, and regular members of the team are reluctant to lead.

Regardless of the nature of the near-crisis, the situation calls for a *pinch hitter*—someone with highly specialized skills who will not be expected to do more than use those skills briefly.

In baseball, that describes the function of a substitute batter, called to the plate late in the game when a particular situation calls for it, such as a change of pitchers or the perceived need to bench a batter who has been a frequent strikeout victim.

Many situations have demanded *pinch hitters* for special tasks. As a result, the baseball term is applied to anyone called on to sub-stitute for an entertainer or speaker who fails to make it to the plate as scheduled.

PIPE DOWN

Big sailing vessels required large crews, since most work was done by hand. The noise from wind and waves made it difficult to transmit orders by shouting. So the boatswain used a special pipe whose notes could usually be heard even in a storm.

When a master wished to give special instructions or give a crew an opportunity to voice complaints, the boatswain piped "All hands on deck." Another signal was used to send men to their quarters below deck. Sometimes a harsh captain would break off discussion and signal the boatswain to pipe the crew down. Failure to obey could be interpreted as mutiny, so rebellion was rare.

Long used literally in the lingo of the sea, the expression was adopted and modified at the U.S. Naval Academy. About 1890 it became customary for a man in his third or fourth year to command a plebe, *Pipe down!* Instead of being an order to go to quarters, this was a demand for silence, and today we treat it as slightly milder but nearly equivalent to "Shut up!"

PIPE DREAM

Should you come up with a really novel idea or plan, chances are that those who first hear of it will pooh-pooh it as a *pipe dream*.

In its earliest decades, the pipe dream was so far out that it seldom made contact with reality. That's because it was produced by opium, brought to England and Europe by merchants who penetrated the Orient and began peddling the stuff yielded by some kinds of poppies.

Pipe dreams influenced several notable literary figures, with Samuel T. Coleridge being high on the list. But by and large, fantasies produced by opium were *pipe dreams* and nothing more.

PIT STOP

The advent of the automobile created a need for a special kind of pit, or hole in the ground. Heavy-duty hydraulic jacks with which to lift cars had not come into vogue. In order to make repairs or give a grease job, a mechanic could wriggle about on his back—or crawl into a pit.

At the Indianapolis raceway, the place where mechanics worked had little in common with the corner service station, but the familiar name stuck to it. To a driver needing fuel or new tires, a *pit stop* was essential even though it meant the loss of precious seconds.

Importance of the pit stop at the Indy 500 and later races added color and variety to everyday speech. As a result, an interstate highway traveler in desperate need of a toilet or a cup of coffee is likely to make a *pit stop* at a place that has no pit.

PLAY FOR KEEPS

Human nature being what it is, differences in personality often emerge very early. When marbles were high on the list of favorite toys for children, many bouts ended by sorting them out so everyone could go home with the ones that were brought.

But there was another and a far more serious kind of play. Before starting it, opponents agreed that all marbles captured during competition would become the property of the winner. Any boy or girl who put a bag of marbles at risk was likely to have a little thicker skin than run-of-the-mill players—a competitor to be avoided by all except those also willing to *play for keeps*.

PLAY HOOKY

Isaak Walton, one of the most widely read early writers about fishing, stressed the importance of getting the hook fixed firmly in the mouth of a fighting fish. His followers, conscious that this required a sudden jerk of the line, began to use *hook* as a verb of action. A person who decamped hastily was said to *hook it*. Charles Dickens used the phrase in this sense.

Compulsory education gave some youngsters an incentive to *hook it* in a new way. When a teacher's back was turned, a truant would bolt off. If this ruse was successful, a student was likely to hide out the next day and fail to appear for roll call.

Adolescents and children being what they are, it became taken for granted that nearly every student would skip school at least once. But even when performed as deftly as a fisherman's master stroke, the jerk of defiance doesn't always work. Parents and teachers know all the ropes, having learned them in their own days of *playing hooky*.

PLAY POSSUM

Imagine that you are a member of a group whose leader asks for volunteers. You aren't interested in the project or don't have time to get involved. What is the best course of action? Sneak hurriedly out of the room? Suddenly become involved in conversation with a friend? Or sit very still, act as though you didn't hear, and *play possum*?

Any veteran woodsman will advise the last alternative. That is because pioneers discovered three hundred years ago that a native-American animal has traits like few others. White men called the creature *opossum,* in an attempt to imitate the speech of Native Americans. Only purists used that name, though; most persons clipped it to *possum.*

Captured, a possum shows great skill in pretending to be dead. Even stroking or shaking seldom causes it to open its eyes. So when a person does a good job of *playing possum*, he or she is—for the moment—dead to challenges or suggestions.

PLAY SECOND FIDDLE

Most early viols, or fiddles, were small and high pitched. They were used along with the lute and timbrel as early as the fifteenth century. But the instrument didn't come into its own until Claudio Monteverde began using it in seventeenth-century orchestral pieces. By the time first- and second-violin arrangements became common, the musician who played first violin was the most honored member of the orchestra.

Popular music followed much the same course as classical, with the person who played the first fiddle taking the leading role.

Even though he or she may not know one musical note from another, any person in a subservient role is said to *play second fiddle*—or follow behind.

PLAY THE FIELD

Horse racing, "the sport of kings," attracts persons willing to take a risk. Anyone wanting some of the action, confident of having picked a winner, is likely to bet on only one animal.

Persons less sure or more cautious like to spread both risk and opportunity. Often that means placing a wager on half the horses in a race. With luck, winnings will be larger than losses when money is spread throughout the field.

Action in the realm of male-female relationships can be even more risky—and potentially more rewarding—than choices made at the pari-mutuel window. Here, too, some are bold enough to concentrate on a sure thing, while others *play the field* in order to hedge their bets.

PLUG AWAY

Given a long and perhaps monotonous job, one person may quit in disgust. Facing the same chores, another person will *plug away,* day after day, until the end is reached.

Speech compares anyone in the latter category with a run-of-the-mill horse. Unlike a splendid racer who gave everything it had for a limited time and then was put out to pasture, the *plug horse* sometimes devoted an entire life to pulling a hackney cab or a dray. After a decade of such work, an animal's steps were likely to be slow and plodding.

Probably named from typical noises made in walking, the plug horse had it all over the racehorse in one respect. A plug kept on going, year after year, until a contemporary racer's productive life was long surpassed. Which suggests that a person who *plugs away* at a task may eventually reach a point that a fiery enthusiast never glimpses except from a distance.

POINT-BLANK

Anglo-Saxon bowmen were among the first to develop a standard type of archery range. They used a flat target whose center was probably marked by a cross section of a tree limb, sawed into a disk, and pegged in position. This white bull's-eye contrasted sharply with the body of the target and was the goal of expert marksmen. Eventually the blank spot was standardized at about the size of a crown piece. Even with the famous longbow, introduced by the Normans who conquered the island kingdom, it was difficult to hit the bull's-eye at any distance. Yet every boy with his first bow knew that in order to hit the target at all, he had to try for the blank.

It became customary to speak of close-range shooting as *point-blank fire,* and with the advent of firearms the term was attached to the use of the new weapons. *Point-blank* came to signify the limit of distance through which a trajectory remains approximately straight. Because such firing in gunnery is destructive, by extension the word came to mean "blunt" or "brutal" as in the expression *point-blank accusation.*

POLL

Hardly a week goes by without the announcement of results from a Harris poll, a Gallup poll, or any other poll commissioned by a news magazine or television network. Many politicians place more credence in polls than they do in their own convictions gleaned from years of experience. Techniques that users consider to be scientific have made poll results newsworthy, regardless of the topic.

This modern activity, which may have impact upon public opinion, is rooted in practices of ancient Britain. There the early census-takers didn't ask a bundle of questions. They simply counted heads, or *polls*, in order to learn how many people lived in a town or borough.

This means that even when conducted by telephone and tabulated by computer, in its literal sense a *poll* is simply a count of heads.

POOH-BAH

Behind the back of a VIP, some associates may refer to the dignitary as a great *Pooh-bah*. This fun-poking title for an important person believed to be keenly aware of his or her importance sounds rather oriental, doesn't it?

That's precisely what a noted English playwright hoped theater-goers would think.

In 1885, William S. Gilbert and Arthur Sullivan offered what many consider their greatest comic opera, *The Mikado*. The setting of the piece required generous use of expressions that would sound as though they came from the Far East. Gilbert coined "Pooh-Bah, Lord-High-Everything-Else," as the special title for one of his characters.

Though not remotely like any term of respect ever used in China, *Pooh-bah* has such a distinctive quality that it entered general speech to designate any notable judged to be a bit of a blowhard.

POOPED

Lots of people find themselves *pooped* at the end of a hard week. Some manage to function when feeling this way most or all of the time. Don't go searching in the bathroom or barnyard for the background of this term. We use it today because our ancestors took to the sea for most of their long-distance journeys.

Englishmen headed toward the New World found that violent waves did most damage when they crashed against the stern, or *poop*, of a vessel. Strong winds and turbulent water could last for weeks. Any ship that lurched out of a long bout with nature was sure to be badly pooped—lucky to be afloat after days of pounding.

Sailors who described the splintered stern of a ship to buddies in the tavern or to family at home frequently confessed that they felt as *pooped* as their vessel looked. Landsmen who heard the seagoing expression borrowed it and put it to use. As a result, we still turn to it in order to describe our feelings in times of total fatigue.

PORK BARREL

Salted pork, packed in barrels, was once basic to the diet of seamen. Sailing vessels often ran out of every other staple food. Generally known to include more fat than a comparable quantity of mutton or beef, a slab of pork near the bottom of a barrel was likely to be found floating in lard.

Abundance of fat near the butt of a sailor's pork barrel led keen-witted American politicians of the nineteenth century to adopt the container's name. At Tammany Hall and other centers of power, men used it disparagingly to name an appropriation made by opponents—but never applied it to the fat-filled bills they sponsored.

Everyday speech borrowed from political talk, with the result that *pork barrel* came to label any enterprise in which funds or jobs are dispensed without accountability.

POSSE

Novels and movies about the American West have made *posse* a household word. However, it had won a respectable place in the vocabulary of crime and punishment much earlier.

No peace officers of modern times even approach the authority of a medieval English sheriff. He was vested by the crown with power to repress riots and other disturbances, no matter what their nature or extent. In a time of emergency, this officer could employ the full power of his county—designated as *posse comitatus* in legal documents of the era. Such a body consisted of every able-bodied man above the age of fifteen, except clergy and noblemen. Riding at the head of this motley and disorganized body, a sheriff often acted in high-handed fashion. Yet as late as 1765, when Blackstone began his famous commentary on the law, the English posse remained a standard instrument of law enforcement.

Settlers in America applied the name of the sheriff's legal band to all self-constituted bodies of citizens who took the law into their own hands.

POSTHASTE

Rapid transmission of important messages has been a matter of concern since early times. Royal couriers were organized by such diverse peoples as the Chinese, Incas, and Persians. Before the beginning of the present era, the Romans had elaborate systems to handle imperial letters. Ordinary folk could not avail themselves of such facilities though.

Under leadership of the University of Paris, the world's first public mail service was launched in the thirteenth century. Men and horses were kept at special places; from Latin for "station," such a point was called a *post*. The English borrowed the post system and used it first for transmission of the king's packet. The spread of education pro-duced many more persons who could read and write letters, so by

1635 the post was so widely used on the island that regular rates for public correspondence were established.

Those who wrote letters considered them important, and they were always eager to speed them on their way. Hence, it became customary to write across the face of a letter, "Haste, post, haste!" Thus *posthaste* came to mean "in a hurry"—whether connected with letters or not.

POTLUCK

Medieval gentry usually had plenty of rich food, frequently serving four or five kinds of meat at a meal. But families in the lower economic classes had no such abundance. Often a struggle was required to get enough food to prevent hunger.

In order to stretch her food, the wife of a commoner would keep an iron pot on an open fire. She threw all her leftovers into it each day and kept it simmering much of the time. If a relative arrived unexpectedly, he was likely to have to eat from the pot without having any idea of what odds and ends had gone into it.

This early and literal form of taking *potluck* came to name the act of eating any meal for which the host or hostess has made no special preparation.

POWWOW

Unless it is strictly formal and conducted under parliamentary rules, a conference or discussion is likely to be called a *powwow*.

Among the Algonquin Indian tribes, a *powwow* was the medicine man who heard voices and saw visions. The powwow frequently presided over councils and rituals and was known as the dreamer.

Europeans learned that such men were often in charge of tribal talk sessions but stumbled over their native title. Garbled into the form of *powwow*, that title was adopted by whites to designate any gathering that involves an idea person.

PRETTY PENNY

Perhaps you grew up in a region where the English influence upon American speech is still strong. If so, you may have heard relatives or friends who want something to say of it, "I'd give a *pretty penny* for that!"

Since the ordinary one-cent piece is not especially pretty, the expression hints at a story.

Long ago, there really was a pretty penny—a gold piece coined in 1257, valued at twenty shillings. Subjects of King Henry III, who had the coin issued, didn't like it. Like the U.S. two-dollar bill, it wasn't well suited for commerce. So no additional gold pence were coined by later rulers.

For several centuries, a tradesman might occasionally see one of King Henry's pieces. In addition to their face value, they came to be prized as good-luck pieces. One of these shiny gold coins was both valuable and pleasing to the eye. So it became customary to speak of any prized article as being worth a *pretty penny*.

Obsolete so long that it is seldom found even in a valuable collection, the thirteenth-century coin retains a tenuous hold in American speech after more than seven hundred years.

PRIMA DONNA

A person doesn't have to be an entertainer in order to be known among colleagues as a *prima donna*. Anyone may gain the title, if others conclude that he or she is overly temperamental or conceited.

This usage is Italian, pure and unadulterated.

Literally meaning "first lady," it has been employed for centuries as a title of respect for the leading female member of an opera company. Like some stars of today, the prima donna was granted special privileges and perks, which, combined with rave reviews on her talent and beauty, could make her vain and demanding.

At least twenty years ago, many of our ancestors decided that it was better to have as little as possible to do with the first lady of a visiting opera company. Adopting the title bestowed on her at home, unchanged in spelling, they began using it in a derogatory sense. Once started, it soon became widely used throughout the English-speaking world.

PULL A FAST ONE

Should someone try to *pull a fast one* on you, take charge. Look at details carefully and insist that sales talk or shuffled papers be slowed down. If you don't, there is a good chance you will lose.

That is probably what happened many times, during or soon after the 1920s.

Many an obscure baseball pitcher seemed mediocre until a moment of crisis. That's when he would *pull a fast one*—hurling a ball at such speed that the batter would be caught off guard. Another deception centered on movements of a dancer. Using a confederate, or shill, many a sharpster shuffled clumsily for maybe ten or fifteen minutes. When onlookers were persuaded to wager about his skill, he would *pull a fast one*. That is, he would move his feet so fast it was impossible to follow them.

Emulating the baseball pitcher who suddenly develops blistering speed, and maybe the shuffle dancer as well, there are folks who will try to *pull a fast one*—or get away with a smooth swindle—in almost every area of activity.

PULL ONE'S LEG

Anyone who sets out to *pull your leg* will have a prank or practical joke in mind. Though the expression makes a lot of sense, its original meaning was far from funny.

Thieves operating in London's underworld didn't roll their victims until modern times. Instead, a mugger worked in partnership with a tripper-up. This rogue used wire or rope or a walking stick to trip pedestrians who ventured into an alley. Once a victim was prostrate, an accomplice of the tripper-up stripped him of valuables.

Since footpads really did pull the leg of a person in the process of tripping, their actions created a phrase used to name any mishap leading to stumbling. Over a period of centuries, it came to be applied to the practice of making fun by causing someone to betray ignorance. This means that the victim of a modern tripper-up isn't likely to be robbed of a wallet or a purse—but may lose his or her temper.

PULL STRINGS

Anytime a deal is pending, it helps a lot to have a friend who knows how to *pull strings*. We use this expression to indicate use of influence because string-pullers were among the earliest popular entertainers.

No one knows where the art of puppetry originated, but it reached an early peak in France. A veteran performer could make a marionette—or "little Mary"—execute movements so complicated that it seemed to be alive.

Most spectators knew that a showman pulled the strings that made the puppet bow or dance. Since the hands of the puppeteer were out of sight, his actions were compared with behind-the-scenes manipulation of any sort, and a long-lasting expression was born.

PULL THE PLUG

If financiers or authorities *pull the plug* on a project, there is a good chance it will go down the drain. Still, this way of expressing the idea of bringing something to an end is not indebted to round rubber plugs used in old-fashioned bathtubs.

Rather, it was the pulling of an electrical plug from an outlet that gave rise to the phrase. Borrowing from everyday experience, early in the electrical age it became common to express the idea of termination by using the phrase spawned by bringing early appliances and machines to a halt.

PULL THE WOOL OVER ONE'S EYES

Only a few centuries ago, most men of importance wore large wigs. Since judges were especially dignified, they adopted appropriately prominent wigs.

Regardless of how skillful its maker, a woolen transformation for the head was likely to be clumsy. Many of them slipped in use, temporarily blocking vision.

A typical lawyer who succeeded in tricking a judge bragged and laughed simultaneously at having *pulled the wool over his eyes*. Use in legal circles was so common that the expression came to stand for any ruse leading to deception.

PULL UP STAKES

A person restless at work and not happy with the climate or job opportunities may be ready to *pull up stakes* and go elsewhere.

This expression, from a commonly told tale, owes its existence to Phineas T. Barnum's great American circus. Seldom spending more than two or three nights in one location, the circus was performed in tents whose ropes were secured by stakes driven into the ground. When the circus left town, *pulling the stakes up* came to be synonymous with "moving."

Though it sounds great, that explanation is a long way off target. When public land in the West was grabbed by a homesteader, he was expected to stay within survey lines marked by stakes. But many a greedy fellow went out after dark, pulled up the stakes, and relocated them to suit himself.

Legality of such action was rarely challenged. Today, a person who wouldn't know a boundary marker if he met it in the middle of the street is said to *pull up stakes* when an old location is abandoned in favor of a new one.

PULLMAN

Overnight sleeping cars drawn by locomotives derived their name from that of their inventor, George Mortimer Pullman.

It took a long chain of events to put his surname into the stream of speech. Pullman experimented in building cars for sleeping just before the Civil War, but he couldn't sell his idea. Though he had no success, he couldn't turn the idea loose. Back in Chicago after a stint as a storekeeper in a Colorado mining town, he invested twenty thousand dollars—everything he had—and eventually completed the costly and luxurious Pioneer.

Everyone acquainted with the Pioneer agreed that not only was it ornate and elaborate, but it was actually comfortable. Still, the novel railroad car wasn't well suited for overnight use. Unfortunately, in order to get the space he wanted, Pullman had built his car too high to get past station platforms or under many bridges. It was shunted onto a siding where it collected dust for two years.

Then, in 1865 President Abraham Lincoln was assassinated, and his cortege carrying him back to Springfield, Illinois, brought out the finest railroad equipment in the nation. The slain president's home state brought out its elaborate Pullman palace car. At great expense, workmen hastily cut down station platforms and raised bridges for the run from Chicago to Springfield. Such an impression was made on visiting dignitaries that President U. S. Grant requested to ride in a Pullman on a subsequent trip from Detroit to Chicago. Hasty changes by the Michigan Central Railroad cleared its line for the oversize car. Its surge in popularity made the sleeping car so familiar that its name is still widely known, despite the fact that few persons of the third millennium have ever spent a night in a *Pullman*.

PUSSYFOOT

An old and almost plausible tale says we use *pussyfoot* to express the notion of care and hesitancy because of a law-enforcement officer.

There seems actually to have been a marshal named Johnson who operated in Oklahoma's Native-American territory for years. He gained a wide reputation for skill in sneaking up on lawbreakers, especially those who ignored statutes governing the use of whiskey. Johnson's movements, almost feline in nature, caused friends and foes alike to call him "Pussyfoot." His activities, according to legend, put his nickname in general speech.

Truth is, many decades before W. E. Johnson earned his nickname, lovers of cats wrote poems praising the stealth of these agile animals. It took only a smidgen of imagination to compare an evasive or extra-cautious person with a stealthy cat and say that any hesitant person is likely to *pussyfoot* around an issue.

PUT THE BEE ON

Settlers along the Atlantic Coast of North America were delighted to find wild bees plentiful. When the household cook needed a sweetening agent, the father or one of the older boys could almost always find a bee tree. The settlers noticed that the tiny insects always worked in groups, and they began to call any communal gathering that combined work and pleasure a *bee*. Ladies had their spinning bees and quilting bees, men their husking bees, and entire communities had spelling bees.

Money was scarce on the frontier, so when churches were organized, congregations were seldom able to give the preacher a cash salary. Instead, they organized *bees* for him. All members of the community, whether they attended church or not, were solicited for gifts of work, clothing, or food.

Sponsors of a bee were not slow to put pressure on reluctant contributors. The result was that any person who made a determined request for a gift was said to *put the bee on* his victim. Later the term expanded to include persistent demands for loans and personal favors as well as gifts.

PUT THE SCREWS TO

In today's high-pressure world, it is common to see a corporation *put the screws to* a competitor. Reasons for doing so range from plans of a takeover to forcing a rival into bankruptcy. Whatever the motive behind the action, and regardless of how it is done, the phrase describing it comes from an era in which torture was common practice.

No jailer was worth his salary until he learned how to use thumbscrews. Fastened upon a captive whose hands were strapped to his sides, these instruments of torture were tightened slowly.

A sudden and abrupt turn of a screw might make a person pass out from pain and thus be unable to confess or tell where loot was hidden.

Today, actual thumbscrews are seen only in museums. Yet it is still an everyday practice for a wheeler-dealer of some sort to *put the screws to* a business or industry in order to try to get something from it.

PUT UP YOUR DUKES

"Put up your dukes!" is a challenge that echoes through the American saga from Revolutionary days to the present. Even on the frontier, the expression borrowed from the English was widely used. Yankees who borrowed the term probably didn't know that it was a tribute of sorts to a son of the king whose forces fought against our founding fathers.

Frederick Augustus, second son of King George III, held many properties and titles including earl of Ulster and duke of York and Albany. A sportsman, duelist, and commander of his father's army, he was so widely admired that bare-knuckle fighters dubbed their fists *dukes of York*.

With the geographical designation dropped as it crossed the Atlantic, the pugilist's tribute was adopted by Colonials as, simply, *dukes*.

QUOTA

Medieval rulers didn't find it easy to raise the funds they needed. It was a simple matter to decide on a desired total, but in order to collect it, specific portions had to be assigned to various divisions of the kingdom. The portion of a tax levy assigned to a city or county was called its *quota*, from a Latin term meaning "what part."

Quota systems proved so effective that they were adopted by military leaders. In 1795 the English Parliament passed a famous quota bill that listed the exact number of men to be furnished to the Royal Navy from every county and even every port of the nation. Draft quotas imposed by Washington during the Civil War led to the most serious protest riots of the period, the best known of which brought widespread destruction and looting to New York City.

American businessmen applied the military expression to their sales territories, and it became commonplace to assign a *quota* to each salesperson who was given a territory.

RACK ONE'S BRAIN

Since the beginning of modern times, Dutch craftsmen have been noted for skill and ingenuity. One of them invented a device used for stretching leather in the process of tanning. From terms conveying the idea of drawing out or stretching, it was given a name that later took the form *rack*.

Civil authorities borrowed racks from tanners and adapted them for use in questioning suspects. With wrists tied to one roller and ankles to another, a wretch who was stretched on the rack could literally be torn apart.

No other method of torture was more effective or more widely used. All civilized nations eventually outlawed the instrument adapted from the leather trade, but by the time it became obsolete it had made a lasting impression upon speech. Consequently, to *rack your brains* in search of an answer is a form of mental torture.

RAIN CATS AND DOGS

If you're caught in a downpour accompanied by thunder and lightning and high wind, there is a good chance that you'll report having seen it *rain cats and dogs.*

These domesticated animals, and no others, are linked in speech with a furious storm. Some scholars think they know why. They point out that witches credited with causing storms often rode the winds in the form of black cats. And in Norse mythology, the god of storms was described as being surrounded by dogs plus their wild cousins, wolves.

Undocumented conjecture suggests that Norse mythology is the seedbed from which the modern phrase has grown.

Another guess, equally plausible, is rooted closer to home. Every furious gale, heard with a sensitive ear, sounds a lot like a sudden eruption of a dog-and-cat fight. Many householders used to keep half a dozen dogs and two or three sets of cats. Perhaps comments that the "storm sounds just like cats fighting with the dogs" were turned into the metaphor crediting heavy clouds with *raining cats and dogs.*

RAISE CAIN

No other volume compares with the King James Version of the Bible in its influence upon speech. Its impact was especially great in the late eighteenth century, when religious leaders turned to Scripture for rules to govern every area of life.

Most parents of the era were strict with their children, yet a lax or indifferent father would let his youngsters run wild. Neighbors usually took it upon themselves to give a bit of advice in such cases. After making a pointed reference to the biblical story of the first murderer, the adviser would declare that Adam and Eve were largely responsible. After all, they reared the boy who became the killer of his brother Abel.

According to this reasoning, any careless parent was likely to raise another Cain. Since the killer's name was synonymous with trouble and grief, a person who creates a disturbance by actions ranging from rearing an unruly child to making a disturbance is said to *raise Cain*.

RANT

England experienced a great deal of trouble during the first half of the seventeenth century. The famous Gunpowder Plot in 1605 warned of growing tensions in the government. Sir Walter Raleigh was executed, and the Duke of Buckingham was assassinated, after which civil war broke out in 1642. After a decade of bitter fighting, Oliver Cromwell overthrew the throne and established the Commonwealth.

Religious differences were almost as great as political ones. Fanatical sects, often violently opposed to one another, competed for popular support. Among these groups was a party of extreme radicals who withdrew from the Seeker movement. They embraced pantheistic doctrines and held public meetings of the evangelistic type. Preachers of this persuasion pitched, snorted, and raved. As English seamen had recently borrowed a vivid Dutch term for "talking foolishly," it seemed appropriate to call these loud fellows *ranters*.

Although the movement dissipated in less than a century, it made a lasting impact upon everyday speech. From this time forth any loud and incoherent speaker, whether behind a pulpit, mounted on a soapbox, or standing flat on the pavement, has been said to *rant*.

RATFINK

Most of us want nothing to do with a dirty *ratfink* who spills things told in confidence. Anyone branded with that label should be avoided.

That was precisely the case, according to southern tradition, with German-born Albert Fink. As the head of detectives who worked for the Louisville and Nashville Railroad, he is supposed to have sent men to infiltrate unions when strikes were in the air. Fink's man—naturally called a *Fink*—sat still, listened quietly, then ratted on fellow workers. Workers wanted nothing to do with such a fellow or his supervisor. Hence *ratfink* came to designate any squealer, scab, or breaker of confidences.

That would be believable—if only the L&N had records of having employed Albert or some other Fink as chief detective. Lacking verification, the story smells like an attempt to explain how a *Pink* who worked for pioneer private eye Allan Pinkerton was transformed into *Fink*.

READING BETWEEN THE LINES

Simple methods of writing in code were devised long ago. Both Julius Caesar and Charlemagne sent battle reports in cipher. But the rise of cryptography as a science dates from the sixteenth century.

Rulers, diplomats, military leaders, and business executives adopted the practice of writing in code. Some personal papers of England's Charles I were so obscure that they were not deciphered until about 1850.

To a person ignorant of the code, a secret paper was meaningless. Ordinary folks fascinated with this mystery concluded that the meaning was not in lines of gibberish, but in the space between them. Writing between lines with invisible ink strengthened this notion.

Except among intelligence agencies, interest in secret writing eventually waned. But language had already been enriched. Spawned from literal views of cryptographs, *reading between the lines* came to suggest the finding of inferences in any document.

READ THE RIOT ACT

Nearly every frustrated parent and employer has been known to *read the riot act*. This in spite of the fact that a solitary culprit rather than a mob of rioters may be the target of wrath.

King George I of England had to deal with a house full of sometimes cantankerous children. But his real troubles were with his subjects. They created so much commotion that in 1716 he issued a proclamation. Any time twelve or more persons engaged in a demonstration, officers of the law were required to read a specified portion of the act and send the rioters home.

Only the very rash continued to push and shove or to yell after the king's edict was proclaimed. A fellow who ignored it could be sent to a penal colony for the rest of his life. In the early decades of the Georgian era, voices were lowered and fists were unclenched fast whenever the riot act was read.

REAL MCCOY

Kid McCoy, now largely forgotten, was among the most colorful boxers of the 1890s. Outside the ring, he didn't look at all formidable. Persons who saw him for the first time often insisted that he couldn't possibly be the noted mauler.

Tradition asserts that mild-looking McCoy fired up when challenged to prove his identity. Barflies who refused to believe him were likely to wind up flat on their faces in the sawdust.

Kid McCoy's memorable demonstrations that he was the real

fighter and not a look-alike created many legends. As a result, a person indisputably the authentic article is likely to be lauded as the *real McCoy*.

RED-LETTER DAY

Even if your engagement calendar is an arrangement of black lines and numbers against a white surface, it is likely to include a *red-letter day* or two.

We use that label for the start of a vacation, a birthday, or a holiday because calendars were once produced by hand—and were seldom seen except in monasteries and convents.

Scribes who prepared ecclesiastical calendars fell into the custom of emphasizing saints' days and feasts by listing them with ink made from ocher—a mineral oxide of iron. A quick glance at a calendar hanging on the wall of an abbot revealed days numbered in red. Since each of these involved both anticipation and preparation, its name attached to secular observances or days that are special for personal reasons.

REDNECK

Some of our colorful expressions are all but self-explanatory. When that is true, someone is sure to hunt for and claim to discover an explanation.

That is what a language specialist did years ago. Explaining why almost anyone from the rural South may be called a *redneck*, an analyst said it is because anger makes the neck turn red.

However, the simple truth is that most people who work in the fields wear clothing that provides a loose and open neck. Day after day, rays of the sun reach exposed skin. A broad-brimmed straw hat provides only intermittent protection. After spending twenty-five years planting and cultivating and harvesting, a fellow's neck is likely to get dark brownish red and stay that way.

Because the American South has been, and is, more agricultural than the industrial North, the term *redneck* has come to be associated exclusively with southerners.

RENEGADE

During the Crusades an occasional Christian deserted and joined the Muslim army. Some of these men were greedy for reward while others were fugitives from European justice. In order to be fully accepted by their one-time opponents, such fellows usually adopted the faith of Islam. From a Latin term meaning "to deny," Spanish churchmen framed *renegado* as a label for the man who denounced his faith.

English borrowed the vivid title and modified it to *renegade.* For three or more centuries, the term was commonly used to designate the occasional turncoat who denied his religion for profit. At the same time, it was applied to a deserter of any type.

The term of contempt was on the verge of dying out when it was revived by novelists who wanted a suitably vigorous name for a white man who deserted to the Indians during frontier warfare. Made prominent by western stories and movies, the term *renegade* has entered half the major tongues of the world.

RHUBARB

A good dictionary will tell you that *rhubarb* means a loud dispute or a noisy argument that may be a prelude to a fight. But the book won't give any hint as to why the name of a vegetable with edible stalks is attached to a squabble.

This usage arose from a common practice of stage and movie directors.

Simultaneous shouting of "Rhubarb! Rhubarb!" by numerous extras in a crowd scene creates an impression of angry chaos. Actors who participated in mob scenes adopted the shouted word to name a loud fracas.

RIDE HERD

In the days of fenceless ranching, some cattle were driven only three hundred miles or so to market. Other drives were four times as long.

Cooks and wagon drivers were the lucky ones, comparatively. Their workday extended only from first light to an hour after sundown. Not so the trail riders. To head off stampedes and to round up stragglers was a twenty-four-hour-a-day job.

Cattle usually obeyed, though sometimes they balked before yielding. Today, you don't have to climb into the saddle in order to *ride herd*. Just concentrate upon keeping everyone moving along at home or on the job.

RIDE ROUGHSHOD

In your observation of others, you've probably seen a boss—or a spouse, a parent, or a child—*ride roughshod* over someone. Long ago this involved more than treating a person insensitively or brusquely.

Medieval blacksmiths who experimented with metal learned to make horseshoes of a special kind. Instead of the smooth metal oval used to protect the foot of a draft animal, a war horse might be equipped with shoes that had projecting points or cutting edges for better footing.

When horseshoes were turned into weapons, the course of the empire was not altered; the devices never worked well. A *roughshod* horse was likely to injure its rider's comrades about as frequently as his foes.

But to an injured man lying on the battlefield, the approach of a roughshod stallion was a fearful sight. As a result, any person who is vocally or physically brutal to an opponent already down is said to *ride roughshod* over the victim.

RIDE SHOTGUN

Should you ever be asked to *ride shotgun* on a fund-raising campaign or some other enterprise, you will be expected to keep your eyes peeled for trouble.

That is precisely what the shotgun-toting guard did in the Old West. Usually assigned a seat beside the driver, the fellow who *rode shotgun* paid little or no attention to passengers or to horses. He stayed busy looking for signs of outlaws like Jesse James or for Native Americans, and he kept his weapon at the ready in case it had to be used.

The shotgun rider continues to be a vital member of a team that may face unexpected problems on the way to a goal.

RIGHT DOWN ONE'S ALLEY

Most English cities and towns of long ago had many more narrow alleys than broad streets; most of them still retain that pattern. Except for members of the wealthy gentry, people were more likely to live on an alley than not.

Asked to make a delivery or purchase close to home, it was natural to respond, "That's *right down my alley!*"

This very British expression for "it's close to home" seemed to early Americans just right as a means of indicating "that is something I'm just the person to do!"

RIGMAROLE

Although origin of the title is obscure, *ragman* was the designation applied to a feudal official by a statute instituted by Edward I of England. When he invaded Scotland in 1296, his aides forced all nobles and gentry to sign a ragman's roll as a token of allegiance. Once they finally complied, the king sent couriers all over the country reading these lists. He hoped that announcing the submission of leaders would bring resistance of the ordinary folk to an end.

Whether from weariness or carelessness, Edward's messengers reeled off the names so quickly that they were difficult to understand. Hence, any jumble of words was compared with a flow of names and called a *ragman's roll.*

Streamlined from frequent use, the old term for the loyalty list is now familiar as *rigmarole*—a label for a nearly incoherent jumble of fast flowing words.

RINGLEADER

Dancing was a major recreational device in medieval Europe. There were few commercial amusements, so many folks in the communities turned out for dances.

A majority of popular folk dances began with all participants holding hands in a circle. At a signal the circle was broken, and one person or couple would lead the rest of the ring through traditional figures. A skillful *ringleader* had a place of honor and was very much in demand at social functions of all sorts. Consequently, the dancer's title expanded and is now used to label anyone who leads others— especially if they are engaged in informal or illicit activities.

RITZY

Old-time inns offered travelers a place to eat and to sleep, but little or nothing more. Toward the middle of the nineteenth century, the rise of a new and larger class of wealthy persons created a different clientele. Promoters vied with one another in building elaborate hotels that included dining rooms about which patrons talked.

César Ritz, a Swiss-born hotelier, won international fame by attracting notables to one after another of his institutions in Paris, London, New York, and elsewhere.

As a posh establishment, the Ritz more than lived up to expectations of investors and travelers. That's why we've adapted a Swiss surname and use *ritzy* to label any establishment marked by costly elegance. The word is also used in reference to people and things of an elite, fancy, or sophisticated nature.

ROBOT

The Czech playwright Karel Capek was among the pioneers of twentieth-century science fiction. As part of his "black utopias," works showing the dangers of technological progress, he wrote a play called *R. U. R.* It centers on a group of mechanical monsters that revolt against their makers. Abbreviating a Czech term for a serf or slave, Capek used the word *robot* to designate the imaginary machine-man of his story. At the end, robots, who had been created to serve humans, came to dominate them completely. The term *robot* has now entered numerous languages.

ROLL WITH THE PUNCHES

There is no way to go through life without being on the receiving end of a lot of punches. But you can try to deal with them as a skillful boxer does.

A beginner in the ring may try to slug it out with an opponent, hoping to catch sight of a haymaker in advance and dodge it. Many veterans insist that it is useless to try to avoid blows. Far better, they say, to reduce impact by bending or stepping to reduce the impact of an oncoming padded fist.

So if you adopt a pattern of *rolling with life's punches,* you find you can take a lot of punishment without going down for the count.

ROOKIE

Whatever the sport in which he bears status as a newcomer, the *rookie* owes his odd name to a long and tangled chain of circumstances.

Rural folks of medieval England were greatly interested in a common type of crow known as a *rook*. These big birds nested in colonies and were loud, dirty, and generally disagreeable. Since they frequently occupied the same nest for years, a large rookery was likely to be cluttered with string, bits of cloth, shiny pebbles, and other stolen trinkets.

Farmers, often victimized at the county fair, compared human swindlers with these noisy feathered thieves. A person taken to the cleaners by a gang of rooks was laughingly called *a rookie*. Since he was likely to be young and guileless, the word came to mean any novice or simple fellow. *Rookie* was eventually adopted by sportsmen in the United States as the designation for a raw beginner, first, in professional baseball, and later any professional sport.

RUB THE WRONG WAY

If you are sensitive, it may not take much to *rub you the wrong way*. A thoughtless remark, a challenging look, or inattention to what you just said may be enough to do the trick.

Long ago, it took a different set of actions to spawn the expression.

Wealthy ladies of the Colonial era were proud of their wide-board oak floors. At least once a week, servants wet-rubbed and then dry-rubbed surfaces. Though simple and routine, these tasks involved running mops along the grain of the wood. A careless worker sometimes mopped across the grain, producing streaks on the floor. To her mistress, such cleaning was worse than none.

Vexation at a domestic who *rubbed the wrong way* was common enough to cause the housekeeping phrase to label clumsy or inept dealing with persons as well as with floors.

RULE THE ROOST

If you know anything about Rhode Island Reds or Plymouth Rocks, you have noticed that a flock—or *roost*—of chickens seldom includes more than one male. That is because a rooster comes out of the egg jealous and mean-spirited. He wants all of the hens and spring chickens for himself.

Bigger, stronger, and louder than females who make up his harem, Chanticleer literally rules every member of his roost—so effectively that his conduct gave rise to a phrase that conveys the idea of unchallenged control.

RUMMAGE

Few operations require more skill than that of loading a large ship. There is a vast amount of space, and every part of it must be packed tightly. Otherwise, the motion of the vessel might cause the cargo to break loose and shift, at the least causing damage, at the worst sinking the ship.

Early French shippers adopted a special term for the loading operation. Their word was *arrumage*, related to the ancestor of "arrange," and it was used to indicate the packing of lumber, casks, and other heavy articles in the hold of a vessel. No matter how carefully the job was done, however, experience proved that some of the cargo was sure to get damaged.

Warehouses frequently put such goods to one side until enough accumulated for a special sale. These goods came to be called *rummage*. By the fifteenth century the word was being applied to any collection of goods of low quality. The *rummage* sale has come to be associated with clothing and other items householders sell to earn a little money.

RUN AMOK

During the Age of Exploration, Europeans encountered many strange sights in faraway lands. They then returned home and wrote about their adventures for the amazement of others. A case in point is the Italian account of strange opium-induced actions in Indonesia, which was translated into English in 1519: "There are some of them [under the influence of opium] who . . . go out into the streets and kill as many people as they meet . . . these are called *Amuco*."

Impressed with the vivid scene, the English made use of it in the expression *run amok*, meaning in a frenzy to do violence or to be in a confused state.

SCALPER

Anytime a *scalper* offers you a ticket at a high price, you find yourself negotiating with a person whose title has gone through several transitions.

An early word for a cup-shaped vessel led housewives of ancient Britain to call a shell-shaped bowl a *scallop*. Many vessels were much like the human cranium, so the rounded bone of the head took that name. Transferred from bone to the skin and hair that covered it, the old title became *scalp*.

Development might have halted had it not been for life on the American frontier, where some Native Americans scalped their foes. Fast growth soon led Chicago and other cities to become infested with men who bought unused portions of railroad tickets for resale. These traders in segments of tickets were compared with Indian braves who collected scalps.

Eventually the boom in transportation tickets came to an end. Passing from rail brokers to persons who speculate in tickets to sporting events and the theater, the name of a bloodthirsty trader became fixed as a *scalper*.

SCAPEGOAT

Very early, the black-coated domestic goat became important in Hebrew religion. On the annual Day of Atonement, it was customary for priests to cleanse people of guilt by "laying their sins on the head of a goat." Afterward, the animal was allowed to escape into the wilderness.

Early translators of Scripture were intrigued by the symbolism of the goat that was forced to escape. With the name of the sacrificial animal altered only a trifle, it became a household word.

Whether having two legs or four, black hair or white, any person or creature on whose head blame is heaped is compared with the animal of Palestine and called a *scapegoat*.

SCREAMING MEEMIES

Scanning your working vocabulary for just the right words with which to speak of severe jitters, there is a good chance you may describe this state as a case of *screaming meemies*.

If you use that expression occasionally, or hear it from others, you are indebted to German makers of weapons. During World War II, many an American doughboy was startled half out of his wits at a never-before-heard sound halfway between a scream and a wail. This sound pattern, never forgotten once it was heard, was a by-product of special artillery shells. Allied fighting men used a word that echoed the sound. As if that were not enough, many who heard it retreated into nervous hysteria that took the same vivid title.

As a result, the *screaming meemies* remains a familiar and dreaded condition long after screaming shells of World War II vintage became obsolete.

SCUTTLEBUTT

If you want inside information, forget public relations releases and listen attentively to the *scuttlebutt*. Much of it is meaningless or erroneous, but by mining this vein of talk you may come up with an occasional gem.

Scuttlebutt is half rumor and half gossip, of course. That is because it was first heard when British sailors gathered around a large *butt,* or cask, of water. For no known reason, such a container was nearly always placed close to a vessel's *scuttle,* or hatch with a movable cover.

Crew members who went for a drink of water liked to exchange the latest rumors with their mates, so talk under a scuttle that sheltered a butt became *scuttlebutt.*

SECURITY BLANKET

Charles M. Schulz is famous as creator of the "Peanuts" comic strip and its characters. One of his claims to fame stems from coinage of the phrase *security blanket* to name any tangible object that soothes nerves and confers confidence.

As initially used by the writer-artist, the expression was literal. Linus, one of his characters, often appears holding a corner of a blanket that drags behind. While absence of that blanket means nervous apprehension, its presence symbolizes confidence and poise.

It is probable that, long before "Peanuts," many mothers and fathers noticed that toddlers felt insecure without their favorite blankets. So the concept behind the phrase may be as old as the family. Still, the word pattern that identifies positive emotional effects of having a familiar object in hand may be strictly twentieth century in origin.

SEEDY

Owners of large tracts of land seldom did any work until modern times. Sharecroppers and day laborers got dirty and sweaty in the fields while their employers dressed as gentlemen and lived the life of Riley.

During the seasons when rye, barley, oats, and other grains were being planted, a fellow who spent his days in the fields was likely to be covered with seeds. Derided as being *seedy*, such a rustic was linked with work-worn clothing.

Once the derisive title entered common usage, it came to mean anything run-down, from shacks to individuals.

SEEING RED

If you *see red* once in a while, you're normal—occasional anger is an ingredient in the mix we call living. Do not rebuke yourself for a brief incident that makes you seem like a bull that is being taunted by picadors.

That was the story circulated to explain why a show of temper is linked with red rather than with, say, purple or yellow. Tradition says that red banners or clothing are used by bullfighters in order to infuriate animals.

There is no truth to the story, though it has circulated for many years. Scientific tests have shown that bulls pay no more attention to red than to other colors. It is the waving of fabric or movement of a matador that catches an animal's eye and induces him to charge.

At least one investigator says that the waving of a white cloth will enrage a bull even more quickly than movements of a red cloth. Even if that is gospel truth, it won't affect our everyday speech. For generations to come, our descendants will still be saying that a person who indulges in a visible burst of temper is *seeing red*.

SELF-STARTER

Byron T. Carter of Cartercar fame stopped one day in 1910 to help a lady in distress. Trying to crank her car, he broke his jaw and eventually died from the injury. Largely because of that incident, Cadillac builder Henry Leland gave Charles Kettering an order for four thousand electric starters.

Most engineers said that an electric self-starter for autos couldn't be made. They calculated that a five-horsepower motor would be needed for it; with batteries, a car would be too heavy to move under its own weight.

Kettering adapted an electric motor used on cash registers. With generator, clutch, and storage battery added, his self-starter was used on the 1912 Cadillac. Now anyone could crank the car by pushing a button with the toe of her shoe.

So much wonder was evoked by the *self-starter* that it came to indicate any person capable of getting things rolling at the push of a mental button.

SELLING LIKE HOTCAKES

Newcomers to North America found one of its most versatile plants to be Indian corn, or maize. When dried and ground, corn yielded meal that made fine bread.

An unknown experimenter discovered still another use for cornmeal: batter fried on a griddle yielded a fluffy delicacy that was best while still hot. Frontiersmen said they preferred their hotcakes fried in bear grease, but town folk were partial to pork lard.

Whenever a Ladies' Aid Society put on a benefit, cooks found it hard to keep up with the demand for hotcakes. Their popularity and money-raising power was so great that by 1825 any merchandise that moved in a hurry was described as *selling like hotcakes*.

SERENDIPITY

Maybe you made a simply terrific accidental discovery of some sort in the past. If not, one or several unforgettable experiences might lie ahead of you, for there's nothing quite like making a great find you didn't anticipate and toward which you didn't work.

Horace Walpole was already internationally famous when he

wrote a 1754 letter in which this melodic word appeared for the first time. He'd been reading an ancient fairy tale from Ceylon, earlier called "Serendip." In the story, three legendary princes frequently stumbled across good things they did not anticipate.

The Three Princes of Serendip so excited the imagination of Walpole that he told Sir Horace Mann about it. To the veteran British diplomat, his correspondent suggested that *serendipity* enables a person who's looking for one thing to find something else entirely.

Adopted by Walpole's literary followers, the made-up term filled a gap in language. Especially among scientists and inventors, *serendipity* has paid big dividends so often that the world would be a great deal poorer without its effects.

SHEEPSKIN

For writing material, the ancient Egyptians used papyrus made from reeds growing in the marshes of the Nile River. This was the preferred writing material until around AD 300, when parchment made from the skins of sheep, goats, and other animals took over.

The art of papermaking reached Europe from the East by 1100. By 1500 paper had almost replaced parchment. This coincided with the invention of the printing press. Nevertheless colleges and universities continued to cling to the custom of preparing "gradua-tion parchments." The actual skin of the animal was used as late as the middle of the nineteenth century, and most diplomas were written in Latin. Whether or not he could read the roll of parchment that certified he had won his degree, a college graduate of the era regarded this as one of his most important possessions.

Born as a slang expression for "diploma" among American students, the name *sheepskin* remains alive in spite of the fact that most sheepskins are now machine-printed on heavy paper rather than hand-lettered on parchment.

SHINDIG

Anyone who has ever attended a wild and wooly hoedown in Maggie Valley, North Carolina, knows that it is the square dance capital of the world. Almost any night during the tourist season, you can find a *shindig* in progress at the Ole Stompin' Ground.

If you have ever participated in a rural dance that included a few beginners, you know that a swinging foot can dig into a partner's shin mighty easily. Any veteran square dance caller will tell you that bruised shins show up every Saturday night. Naturally, a carouse that leaves telltale marks on lower legs of the participants is a *shindig* no matter what else it may be.

SHOOT THE BULL

Confined in a pen, two or three bulls are likely to devote much of their energy to bellowing back and forth at one another. Experienced handlers know that the sounds produced, though frequent and loud, pose no threat. They are simply one effect of the way this male animal likes to make all in earshot aware of his presence.

Male humans, voluntarily penned in a room, tend to devote a lot of their energy to idle talk. Like noises made in a cattle pen, their sounds may mean very little—but seldom stop.

Inevitably, a fellow talking too much will be called down for his tendency to *shoot the bull*, while a session in which several talk back and forth constitutes a bull session.

SHOOT THE WORKS

Anytime you decide to go whole hog, or abolish all limits, you are willing to *shoot the works*. Thoroughly respectable though the expression now is, it owes its existence to the gambling table.

Though far from sophisticated, the game of craps remains popular in the electronic age. A player willing to risk everything on one throw of the dice is likely to offer to *shoot the works*. When that is done, there is no second chance; the game is over, and the little cubes have determined a big winner along with maybe three or more losers.

SHORT SHRIFT

Have you ever been accused of giving *short shrift* to instructions from a superior or a lecture from a relative? If you are guilty of having yielded only quick and perfunctory attention to something, you are not giving *short shrift* in its original sense.

From an Anglo-Saxon term for receiving confession, *shrift* named a common activity of priests—hearing of confessions and giving of absolutions. This could be long and tedious in the case of a person with a badly bruised conscience.

That must have been the case with many lawbreakers. But authorities were often more concerned with schedules; when a head was to be chopped off or a noose was to be fitted, the sheriff wanted the show to come off on time. That meant the final confession of a condemned person had to be brief. Hasty confession followed by fast pronunciation of absolution constituted not a normal rite but a short shrift.

So when someone gives you *short shrift*, you receive time and attention of duration and quality similar to the shrift yielded to a felon only minutes away from execution.

SHOT IN THE ARM

Next time you receive a sudden infusion of energy and enthusiasm, there is a good chance that you will tell others you got a *shot in the arm*. To law-abiding citizens, the idea expressed is so general that it crops up every day in the best of circles.

Mood-altering drugs injected by means of a hypodermic needle were first used by physicians. Some employed them, along with adrenalin and other natural stimulants, in everyday practice. A patient suddenly stimulated, without knowing the nature of the drug received, was likely to call the experience *a shot in the arm*. Under such circumstances, the boost in confidence or energy was therapeutic, legal, and commonplace.

SHOWDOWN

In many a search for truth or struggle for supremacy, a crucial moment comes when everyone is ready for a *showdown*. That means quick and decisive action—an act of finality such that there is no appeal.

Like so many other expressions that have never been accurately tabulated, this one entered American speech straight from the poker table. A special kind of play is involved, of course.

Sometimes players will agree that in the next round, all cards will be dealt face up. Pure luck, not skill, determines the winner in such a case. Once the dealer has finished, a glance around the table will determine who holds the winning hand.

This version of poker doesn't have a great deal to recommend it. But *showdown* play has won enough followers to catapult its name into mainstream speech to designate a decisive confrontation or an act of bringing things into the open.

SIDEBURNS

Civil War general Ambrose E. Burnside was almost as dashing a figure as was George Armstrong Custer. In most public appearances, he sported a hat so flamboyant that it took his name. Defying established custom, Burnside shaved his chin smooth while displaying a full mustache and sidebar whiskers.

Thousands of men wore Burnside hats and adopted the Burnside style of facial hair. Reversal of syllables is a common form of word play. Many a dashing fellow who prided himself on his lovely *burnsides* enjoyed turning the name around. Inverted in popular speech, whiskers that imitated those of the general's became *sideburns.*

The vogue for side whiskers has waxed and waned. Since then, the colorful name adapted from that of a general has been used to designate any patch of hair in front of a man's ears.

SIDEKICK

Pickpockets abounded in London and other English cities during the time of Victorian author Charles Dickens. They anticipated modern youth gangs by forming close-knit organizations. A recruit had to go through an apprenticeship, much as though he were in training for an honorable craft.

Pickpockets developed their own slang vocabulary. A *pratt* was a hip pocket; a *pit* was a breast pocket. They used *jerve* to name a vest pocket and *kick* to designate a side pocket in a pair of breeches.

Even a veteran of this special kind of crime was likely to have trouble with a kick. It lay close to a potential victim's leg and was in constant motion. Worldly-wise London merchants learned that money placed there was safer than in any other pocket.

It became proverbial that a fellow who didn't want to lose his bundle should stash it in his *sidekick.* As a result, any faithful partner always at one's side took the name of the trousers pocket that is most resistant to pickpockets.

SILHOUETTE

Any time you see a *silhouette,* the stark appearance of the black outline can serve as a reminder that its name was bestowed in mockery of a penny-pincher.

Étienne de Silhouette became controller-general of France in 1759. Selected because he was considered capable of solving the nation's financial troubles, he went to work with zeal. All of his money-saving proposals were unpopular, but his suggestion that government pensioners receive reduced allowances created a national uproar.

For generations, street artists had offered outline portraits at low prices. Since these represented an extreme example of economy in art, ridicule of the financier caused his name to become attached to them.

SILVER SPOON IN ONE'S MOUTH

Table utensils of silver—sterling or plated—have become commonplace only in recent times. As late as 1800, only the upper classes owned eating utensils of precious metal. Housewives of the middle and lower economic classes had to be content with pewter.

Earlier generations didn't have metal tableware of any sort. That's shown by the word *spoon*, which grew out of the Anglo-Saxon *spon* (chip). Obviously, the earliest spoons were made of wood. Artisans later discovered how to fashion them from horns of domestic animals. Even among the nobility, metal spoons were not in wide use before the Elizabethan Age.

After precious metals came into limited use for table utensils, wealthy persons adopted the practice of giving silver spoons to their godchildren. The gifts were formally presented at the christening ceremonies, which usually took place when infants were only a few days old. That made it natural to refer to one who received such a gift as being born with a *silver spoon in one's mouth*. A few generations of use impressed the phrase so strongly that it came to stand for prosperity or wealth gained by accident of birth.

SKELETON IN THE CLOSET

English physicians eager to learn more about the human body were long under severe restrictions. Until the controversial Anatomy Act was passed in 1832, only the body of an executed criminal could be dissected. Many an early doctor dissected only one cadaver during his career. Naturally, he prized the skeleton highly and didn't want to dispose of it. Yet public opinion warned against keeping it where it might be seen. So the prudent anatomist hung his prize in a dark corner where visitors were not likely to discover it.

Patients weren't complete numbskulls, however. Most knew or suspected that their physician had a *skeleton in his closet*. From this literal sense, the phrase expanded to indicate hidden evidence of any kind.

SKID ROW

It is a paradox of modern American life that there is a *skid row* in every city of a nation famous for its mind-boggling innovations. An unsavory district of an urban area owes its name to the invention of a fast way to get timber to market.

Forestry began in earnest soon after the Civil War. As part of every big logging operation, a track of logs or heavy boards was built from the site of cutting to the nearest road. Often greased with lard, this made it easy to *skid*, or to drag, logs.

In a village near a lumber camp, a street lined with shacks was compared with the chute for dragging and was given its name. By the time large-scale logging began to decline, skid roads of hamlets caused any run-down and disreputable street or section of any city to be known as *skid row*.

SKIN OF ONE'S TEETH

Since no tooth is covered with skin, why on earth do we say that when a person barely misses disaster, he has escaped by the *skin of his teeth*?

The expression comes from the book of Job (19:20) where he describes his narrow escape: "My bone cleaveth to my skin and to my flesh and I have escaped with the skin of my teeth." With these words Job sought to show just how dire was his situation.

Retained in the famous King James Version, the colorful phrase was pounded into everyday speech. Although we have no real skin on our teeth, Job's description is vivid, if exaggerated, and not likely to be replaced with a more accurate phrase.

SLAPSTICK

It was common for an old-time stand-up comedian to do everything possible to milk his audience. When applause was scant and barely audible, such a fellow was likely to give a signal to an aide.

Thoroughly acquainted with the routine and knowing just when to expect the next punch line, the aide would step forward at the right instant. Before some onlookers knew what was going on, he'd give the wooden stage a mighty slap with a heavy stick or thick board. Some persons laughed and others frowned; anyone sleeping was awakened by the thunder of the *slap stick*.

So many performers made such heavy use of the slap stick that the name of the tool designed to put life into a dull routine attached to any broad farce or low-grade comedy.

SLEAZY

A row of cheap condominiums is likely to be recognized as *sleazy* within a few months after having been finished. A tabloid newspaper may get this name before it rolls from the press.

Decades ago, it took a while for potential consumers to be sure that cloth from Germany would not hold up well. A special kind of linen, called *Sleasie* because it came from the Silesian district, served as a come-on for London merchants. Having bought a wagonload of the stuff for nearly nothing, a vendor could offer it at a low price and still make a killing from it.

By the time consumers learned to distinguish *Sleasie* by quick examination, lots of the substandard linen had been sold. Consequently, the cloth name attached itself to anything shoddy or grungy or obviously inferior in quality.

SLIPSHOD

At least as early as the fifteenth century, house slippers came into vogue. Made without heels or fastening devices, they did not damage floors and seemed to be easy on the backs of the wearers. Thin felt was the standard material used in making them.

Slip-shoes, as they were widely called, were designed strictly for indoor use. But careless persons often kept them on their feet when walking near their homes, or even on longer excursions. By 1580, it had become proverbial that a shameless person would go slip-shod to worship.

Many persons who wore slip-shoes into public places were careless about their appearance. As a result, we still use *slipshod* to designate anyone who is slovenly in appearance.

SLUSH FUND

Since refrigeration was far in the future, the food supply was a major problem during the great age of sailing. A seasoned ship's master wouldn't leave port without taking aboard as much salt pork as he could buy.

When fried or broiled, the all-important meat yielded grease in such quantities that special storage vats were used for it. Much waste fat, or *slush,* was used to grease timbers. But on many voyages the stuff accumulated faster than it could be used. Back home after months at sea, a vessel might have hundreds of pounds of slush.

Long-established tradition provided that when a voyage ended, slush was sold in order to buy extras for members of the crew. So widely familiar was this seagoing *slush fund* that its name attached to a sum of money diverted from an operating budget for extras such as bribery or corrupt practices.

SMALL FRY

Our use of *small fry* as a label for children memorializes, in a fashion, speech patterns of long ago. For in eras when most people lived close to the land, animals, birds, and fish were of vital importance. Dependent upon them, humans devised separate names for the stages of life cycles.

A few words from this specialized vocabulary have survived. As a result, first-time visitors to New England see numerous T-shirts proclaiming: "I CAUGHT SCROD IN BOSTON." That notice seems vaguely suggestive of venereal disease, until an outsider learns that a young codfish is a scrod.

Fishermen long referred to immature fish of all kinds as *fry*. Which meant that *small fry* were tiny swimmers indeed. With its background lost in obscurity, the phrase *small fry* is most often applied to small children or unimportant events.

SMELL A RAT

Whether or not you own a dog, chances are good that you've seen a pet suddenly start whining, barking, and scratching at the floor or wall. When that happens, the dog may have smelled a rat.

Civilized man has had few enemies so cunning and persistent as the common rodent. Able to adapt to almost any climate and diet, the rat has been a nuisance since the Stone Age. For centuries, it was a common practice to give terriers and other rat-hunting dogs free run of palaces as well as huts. In the course of a quiet evening, it was not unusual for an animal to spring into action without an obvious cause.

If no other triggering effect could be found, the dog's behavior would be shrugged aside as caused by its having caught a whiff of a rodent. This occurred so frequently that when an event triggers automatic suspicion in a person, that person is said to have *smelled a rat.*

SMELLING LIKE A ROSE

Barnyard humor was probably born a few days after animals were first herded into a pen. Still going strong, this special brand of humor has been a favorite of many famous people, including Abraham Lincoln.

Every rustic likes to pretend that no city slicker has sense enough to identify horse or cow dung. Wandering into a barnyard, a fellow who looks down his nose at rubes is likely to fall flat on his face in the manure pile. That outcome is central to many a barnyard story.

But perhaps for the sake of variety, an occasional spinner of tall tales will use a different ending. In such a yarn a person falls into a manure pile as usual—but emerges from it without a trace of foul odor.

That outcome is always described as a result of extraordinary good luck, not skill or wisdom. So it isn't necessary to remember the one about a son of a president who was up to his neck in a savings and loan scandal to realize that once in a while someone in a scrape really does come up *smelling like a rose.*

SMOKE OUT

King Edward III of England personally led armies that invaded and plundered France. But when he and his victorious warriors returned home, they brought the Black Death with them. Plague broke out in 1348 and soon swept through the kingdom.

Doctors didn't understand the nature of the disease and had no cure. Many agreed with common folk that demons spread the fearful malady.

Everybody knew that there was just one sure way to drive evil spirits out of a house: fill the place with dense smoke. Since demons who brought the plague might linger after victims died, any house visited by the Black Death was likely to be fumigated. Even bed linens and clothing of the dead were carefully smoked.

This practice caused people to say that anyone seeking concealed information is trying to *smoke out* a secret. Such a quest may be as important as purifying a house after the Black Death, but few who follow it nowadays burn sulphur and herbs.

SMOKEY

Anytime you drive into a state where radar detectors are outlawed, you had better keep your eyes peeled for a *Smokey*. These days, he can come at you out of nowhere in an unmarked car.

Don't blame Smokey the Bear if you pick up a ticket. It all started during the decades when the U.S. Forest Service was going all-out for prevention of forest fires. Smokey the Bear became so familiar that he was almost like a member of the family.

Rangers displaying the Smokey symbol wore broad-brimmed hats of a style sported by few civilians. But many a state highway patrol system adopted a hat like that as part of the uniform. A really alert driver doesn't have to watch for the blue light on top of a car. All he or she has to do is spot one of those distinctive hats in order to know that a *Smokey* is on the prowl.

SNOW JOB

When a person sets out to do a *snow job* on you, the temperature does not matter. It can happen in a season when falling white stuff wouldn't last thirty seconds after hitting the ground.

But the verbal metaphor really is based on winter weather. That is when snow can pile up deeply before anyone has a chance to clear a path.

A persuasive flow of words aims at overwhelming by sheer

mass. So be wary when you face a verbal deluge that is too smooth and allows you no time to think about dealing with it. There is a good chance someone is trying to blanket you two feet deep before you can find the old snow shovel.

SOFT-PEDAL

Anytime you try to *soft-pedal* claims of a political party or aspirant for office, your technique is borrowed from music.

When the pianoforte first came on the market, it was regarded as a marvel. The musical instrument's original name, now clipped in half, proclaimed that it produced both soft (*piano*) and loud (*forte*) sounds. It was the radical new soft pedal that made the instrument really distinctive. By use of it, a player could soften notes by a touch of a toe. There is no such handy device with which to de-emphasize claims of an organization or party in which you believe. But a little practice will help you learn how to *soft-pedal* emphases that you judge to be so loud that they are abrasive.

SOUTHPAW

Every *southpaw* realizes that practically everything in modern life is geared for a right-handed person. There's a movement afoot to make some corrections, but an overwhelming preponderance of right-handedness makes progress slow.

All lefties owe the southpaw label to the influence of sports writer Finley Peter Dunne. Dunne captured a huge following during the 1880s and invented several new words, most of which didn't win general acceptance.

But he made a contribution to speech by calling attention to a feature of Chicago's great baseball park. With the home plate lined up directly west of the setting sun, it was the arm south of a line between the mound and home plate that a left-handed pitcher worked.

Dunn labeled such a player a *southpaw*, and the designation caught on. Wide use of it by baseball fans caused it to expand to name any left-handed person, not necessarily ever engaged in hurling baseballs.

SPAM

Executives at the Hormel Foods Corporation, one of the world's foremost meat packers, had a brainstorm in the middle of the twentieth century. Seeking a catchy trade name that could be registered, Hormel offered a one-hundred-dollar prize to the person who could come up with the best name for its canned minced pork product. The winner offered *Spam*.

Spam, still stocked on supermarket shelves everywhere, played a major but little-known role in world events. Nikita Khrushchev paid a special visit to company headquarters in Minnesota to express his personal thanks for the role Spam played in feeding Russian soldiers during World War II, and American GIs will never forget this staple of their undesirable C rations.

Although it may have sustained many soldiers during World War II, after the war Spam got a reputation for being "junk" meat. In the early days of the Internet, vendors began experimenting with advertising through brief messages sent to multitudes of computer users. The popular name for the famous meat packer's "junk" meat soon came to refer to this unwanted, or "junk," e-mail—in a word, *spam*.

SPARK PLUG

Gottlieb Daimler's 1885 auto was equipped with a tiny platinum tube mounted in its single cylinder. Heated by a benzene-fed Bunsen burner, the hot tube-fired gasoline vapors mixed with air.

Seeking more exact control over ignition, inventors developed an electrical gadget. Having a gap of a sixteenth of an inch, it screwed into a cylinder and yielded sparks with conducting current. About the size and shape of a plug used to stopper a barrel, it was natural to call it a *spark plug*.

For years, some drivers and mechanics stuck to hot tube ignition. However, the spark plug eventually became the standard device for firing fuel in a cylinder.

It worked so well that people who prodded things into action were compared with it. Expanded in meaning, *spark plug* now names anyone good at getting an organization or business fired up and ready to move.

SPENDTHRIFT

Common folks of medieval Europe were frequently taxed at a rate which makes our income tax seem mild. As a result, it was difficult for anybody except noblemen to accumulate an estate. When a man did succeed in saving money to be left to his sons, he proudly referred to it as his *thrift*. Some heirs dissipated the thrift of a lifetime in short order. As a result *spendthrift* entered the language as a vivid expression for any type of prodigal.

SPILL THE BEANS

Early Greek secret societies had strict membership requirements. A candidate for admission was voted upon by members. Only a few adverse ballots were required for disqualification.

In order to keep voting secret, white beans were dropped into a container by those who favored a candidate. Brown or black beans constituted negative votes. Only officials were supposed to know how many of these were cast. Occasionally, however, a clumsy voter knocked a jar or helmet over and disclosed its contents. It was embarrassing, to say the least, to *spill the beans* in this literal fashion.

While this is the accepted origin of the phrase, scholars are stumped as to how it entered the English language early in the twentieth century. However, it is a popular phrase naming indiscretion in revealing information of any kind.

SPINSTER

Our word *spinster*, meaning an unmarried woman, is rapidly becoming archaic and is likely to drop out of speech during the twenty-first century.

The term hasn't always had the application now attached to it. The original use applied to the occupation of spinning, which was traditionally a woman's job. In the ninth century, King Alfred spoke of his descendants as those on the spear side and the spindle side—that is, male and female. *Spinster* was widely used as a title of respect for both single and married women until the time of Queen Elizabeth.

Since homemakers with families had to take on other responsibilities, spinning became more and more the occupation of unmarried women. By the seventeenth century, practically all professional spinsters were unmarried. So, in the course of time, it came to be natural that women not likely to marry should be called *spinsters*.

STAND PAT

Several common substances were long patted into shape by hand. This job took more skill than a person watching for the first time might think.

Dexterity involved in patting butter, dough, or potter's clay caused anything apt and clever to be called *pat*.

Poker buffs borrowed the household term and used it to name an original hand not likely to be improved by drawing additional cards. An experienced player dealt the right cards would *stand pat*, or say no when offered more cards.

Whether in a business conference or a meeting of the PTA, a person who has never played poker can *stand pat* by refusing to budge or by resisting even minor change.

STAVE OFF

Widely popular for many decades, the medieval sport of bear baiting was forced into partial eclipse. There simply were not enough animals to supply the demand. So a substitute sport pitted dogs against bulls. A big animal could disembowel a foe with one sweep of its horns, so tips were usually cut off. That enabled savage dogs often to get the better of it.

Once a bull was wounded, its owner liked to drive dogs away. This was not easy, since they were big and fierce. Most refused to stop tormenting a bull until given a smart rap with a staff or a barrel stave.

This occurrence was common enough to create a new phrase. It came to be roughly synonymous with postponement, since a fighting bull wasn't saved from death when his owner *staved off* a pack of dogs. A reprieve was brief; the bull would fight again and again and ultimately be killed. By the sixteenth century, the notion of *staving off* was being applied to death or disaster of any kind.

STEAL THUNDER

For more than two centuries the English-speaking world has used the expression *stealing thunder* to mean the appropriation of any effective device or plan that was originated by someone else.

An obscure English dramatist was father of the phrase. For the production of a play, John Dennis invented a new and more effective way of simulating thunder onstage. His play soon folded, but shortly afterward he discovered his thunder machine in use for a performance of *Macbeth* at the same theater. Dennis was furious. "See how the rascals use me!" he cried. "They will not let my play run, and yet they steal my thunder!"

STEAMROLLERED

Steam provided energy for pumps in England's coal mines for decades before the modern steam engine was developed. After efficient models were devised, they were reserved for heavy-duty use.

Road builders modified an early type of locomotive in order to produce a machine that replaced horse-drawn rollers. Equipped with wide wheels and used for packing roadways and crushing stones, a steamroller was as powerful as many animals. Especially in the United States, but also in Paris and other Old World cities, a glimpse of the road-building machine provided fodder for animated conversation.

Now obsolete, the mechanical monster was one of the most powerful devices of its era. People who saw it in action were so impressed with its relentless advance that we still say a person or movement crushed by overwhelming force has been *steamrollered*.

STEP ON IT

Engineering changes enabled motorists to pick up speed rapidly before World War I. Some models still used hand throttles to regulate the flow of fuel, but most employed the relatively new "foot feed" not yet commonly called the *accelerator*.

Known by whatever name, the foot-controlled mechanism freed both hands for steering. That meant a driver could keep a car in the road even when moving from ten to forty miles per hour in seconds. Reporting such an exploit, a motorist was likely to talk about having stepped on the gas.

Regardless of whether or not you drive a car with a foot feed, when planning to speed up action of any sort it is customary to announce intentions to *step on it*.

STIFF UPPER LIP

For at least a dozen centuries, men of England alternated between shaving and growing whiskers. Razors were used every day during most of the reign of Queen Anne. To make up for what the razor took, many a sporting fellow donned a wig. When wigs were abandoned by most people except barristers, facial hair made a comeback.

Soldiers may have been first to give up beards in favor of mustaches. But military men who grew them discovered a serious drawback. Hair on the upper lip, no matter how carefully clipped and waxed, moves at the slightest twitch of a muscle.

Many a stern old officer, himself slow to adopt the newfangled mustache, roared and pitched. If a young fellow insisted upon growing hair under his nose, he would have to learn to keep a *stiff upper lip.* Movements of a mustache when standing rigidly at attention might even be considered a breach of discipline.

Spreading from barracks talk of men hoping to become known as officers and gentlemen, the phrase came to label self-control in any difficult situation.

STONEWALL

Any person subjected to questioning may decide to be difficult and *stonewall.* This particular expression has undergone more than one transition.

Step one occurred among cricket players. Contestants lauded a successful batsman by congratulating him on having blocked everything as effectively as though he had been a stone wall.

Step two involved Confederate general Thomas J. Jackson. Lauded for having failed to yield ground when under heavy attack by Union forces at Bull Run, Jackson was nicknamed "Stonewall."

A stonewall batsman doesn't let opponents score, and Stonewall Jackson didn't yield under pressure. Therefore, contemporary usage includes *stonewall* as a designation for a delaying tactic such as refusal to answer questions.

STOOL PIGEON

Both in England and on the American frontier, pigeons were an important source of meat for generations. Many were captured by trappers. Others were shot down by hunters, but damaged meat was considered less tasty.

Trappers learned how to use a tame bird, as a decoy to lure wild ones into snares. Many a fellow spent much of the day waiting for game to come, while his decoy was tied to a stool so it couldn't escape.

Such *stool pigeons* were common for many years. Since each of them functioned to entice others into a trap, the name was adopted to designate anyone who betrays colleagues or comrades.

STRAIT-LACED

Should someone describe you as *strait-laced*, your views will determine whether to regard this as complimentary or disparaging. For the old garment term may be interpreted either way.

Rather elaborate corsets were sometimes worn in classical times. But the garment didn't become widely popular until a few centuries ago. In the gilded era that followed discovery of the New World, many great ladies went wild about clothes. For sake of fashion, a grand dame might pull her bodice so tight that her waist seemed to shrink. Since anything tight and narrow was called *strait*, a woman strapped into a whale-bone corset was literally laced strait, or *strait-laced*.

It was inevitable that comparisons should be made. As early as 1526, a person of strict convictions was given the name of a woman laced into a corset so tightly that she could hardly breathe.

STRING ALONG

Almost from the time men first put halters and bridles on animals, strings of them were formed for some operations. Caravan drivers tied as many as fifty camels together in single file then handled them with only two or three men. Long strings of donkeys were linked in pack trains, and smaller groups of horses were driven in the same fashion.

A person who is *strung along* is being led, sometimes by an increasingly long string, and sometimes with an increasingly distant goal. In today's popular usage, *stringing along* has a meaning much similar to "leading someone on," making them believe that a promised resolution is imminent when in fact there is no real intent to quickly deliver said resolution.

STUFFED SHIRT

Farmers have been making scarecrows for centuries. They were designed, of course, to frighten away small animals and other birds in addition to pesky crows.

In order to make a male figure, an old pair of trousers and a shirt were stuffed full of straw. A figure topped by a battered hat would be kept erect by means of a broomstick or a pole. Apparently standing in the field, it just might keep varmints away.

Some persons, even in positions of authority, show few signs of action. Male or female, a human *stuffed shirt* is about as vital—and as commanding in the eyes of colleagues—as a weather-beaten scarecrow guarding a corn patch.

STUMBLING BLOCK

In 1534, when William Tyndale was making one of the earliest translations of the Bible into English, he had difficulty with Romans 14:13. Paul wrote that Christians should not put a *skandalon* in another's path to cause them to fall from grace. The Greek word referred to "a spring of a trap," an unfamiliar item to the English. Tyndale therefore converted the old hunting term into a reference that fitted the experience of his time, coining the term *stumbling block* from having seen people trip over debris scattered in alleys. Later translators of the King James Version used the phrase, and the expression was absorbed into the language as any obstacle or source of error.

STYMIED

Games somewhat like golf have been played since antiquity. It was in Scotland, however, that the modern sport took form. As early as 1450 it had become a craze with Highlanders. The game interfered with archery so seriously that rulers handed down three separate edicts forbidding golf—in 1457, 1471, and 1491.

Public interest was too keen, however, and the law couldn't be enforced. Although golf spread to nearly all civilized lands, some of its most distinctive terms have Scottish origins. *Styme*, an ancient term for "obscure" or "hidden," was used in the situation where one ball on the green blocks the path to the hole of another ball.

When a player is *stymied,* he must choose between losing a stroke and trying to loft his ball over that of his opponent. As early as 1850, it was considered bad form to bring about a stymie on purpose. From the unplanned dilemma on the putting green, a person blocked in any effort is said to be *stymied.*

SUBPOENA

Latin survived the fall of the Roman Empire by many centuries. Recent changes in Roman Catholic patterns of public worship seem likely to cause the classical language to retreat from its last major stronghold. As late as the fifteenth century, Latin was the language of worship, scholarship, and law. Even though a witness to whom it was addressed couldn't read a word of Latin, the document commanding an appearance in court was written in that language.

A person required to appear as a witness or receive a penalty for failure to show up was served a paper that began, *Sub Poena ad testificandum*. In the case of a civil action in which a judge wanted documents produced, the summons read, *Sub poena duces tecum*. In common speech the classical term for "under penalty" was fused into a single word, *subpoena*, that designates a legal summons— even though it may be written entirely in English.

SUNDAE

Numerous stories are told concerning the origin of the ice-cream *sundae*, differing chiefly in tracing it to various American cities. There seems little doubt that the basic account is accurate. Evidence points to Evanston, Illinois, as the city of origin. It seems that around 1875, city fathers passed a law forbidding the sale of ice-cream sodas on Sunday. Someone thought of serving ice cream with syrup but no soda water.

This *Sunday soda* became quite popular, and on weekdays a number of customers asked for *Sundays*. Officials of the city objected to naming the dish after the Sabbath, so the spelling was modified— and *sundae* it has been ever since.

SWAT TEAM

Many acronyms, formed by combining initial letters, are all but forgotten after having been in the news for a period. Not so the title of a modern police unit that operates much like a military assault team.

The rise of terrorism, marked by an increased holding of hostages, enticed U.S. authorities to take a new look at ways of dealing with it. Several national conferences were held, and as a result some cities formed Special Weapons and Tactics units.

Soon it was found that a *SWAT team* equipped with high-powered weapons and elaborate communications devices was useful in many kinds of crises. Perhaps because such a group tends to strike swiftly and swat the opposition firmly, the artificially formed word that names it has become firmly entrenched in modern speech.

SWEETHEART

During the era when the longbow was the ultimate weapon, even physicians knew little about human anatomy. Pumping action of the heart caused it to be regarded as the seat of personality. Expressions paying tribute to this notion were probably literal rather than figurative. A person could be hard-hearted, soft-hearted, light-hearted, or heavy-hearted.

In this climate of thought and speech, it was natural for a lover to refer to one who made the heart beat faster as *swete hert*. Separate terms were hyphenated for two or three centuries before *sweetheart* entered modern talk to label the sweet person who makes the heart throb.

TABOO

Europeans who ventured into the South Seas during early voyages of exploration were intrigued by colorful native customs. Some of the most puzzling were those that forbade passage or contact. Among the Tongans, it seemed that everywhere a seaman turned, he was confronted by a priest who barred his way and muttered: "*Tabu! Tabu!*" (Forbidden! Forbidden!)

No forbidden object could be touched, or even examined from a distance, and a forbidden place could not be entered.

Famous explorer Captain Cook and other sailors altered the Polynesian term a trifle and returned home with the novel sound that expressed warning. Several classical and European words indicating caution were supplanted by the novel expression from the South Seas.

As a result, to speakers of numerous modern languages, anything forbidden is now likely to be termed *taboo*.

TAILSPIN

Early planes sometimes tipped sharply downward then went into a combination roll and yaw—or turn about the vertical axis. Engineers who studied the complex action called it *auto-rotation*. Airmen rejected that big word in favor of *tailspin*, even though it was the entire plane and not just the tail that spun.

Until 1916, no pilot came out of a tailspin without a crash. Caught in one that year, the great Eddie Stinson decided he might as well die quickly—so he pushed the stick forward. To his amazement, the rate of spinning slowed and he regained control. After that, barnstormers often performed tailspins to thrill crowds.

Risk of an involuntary downward spiral has been all but eliminated from aircraft. Yet the hazard faced by aviation pioneers left a legacy in language. Whether arguing at a cocktail party or asking for a raise, a person threatened with a loss of self-control is still said to go into a *tailspin*.

TAKE THE BULL BY THE HORNS

Many a cowboy was as tough as those depicted in movies and television. No sport was considered very worthy unless it involved some danger. Yet some grizzled horsemen hesitated when challenged to wrestle steers. It was useless to grab the legs or neck of a feisty young male, attested the veterans of these contests. In order to win, the human challenger had to seize an animal's horns. Gripping them firmly, with skill and luck a fellow could throw his four-legged opponent to the ground before being gored. Cow camp recreation enriched general speech. Anyone who wades head-on into an opponent or a problem is said to *take the bull by the horns*.

TALK A BLUE STREAK

Tall tales were the stock in trade in early American yarn-swapping at the general store or tavern. Possibly from the influence of lightning, often having a bluish hue, fast movement was widely known as a *blue streak*.

What, if anything, moves as rapidly as the human tongue?

An excited person can jabber almost as fast as lightning stabs through the skies. But rapid speech is no more exhausting to listeners than is the slower-paced chatter by someone who talks endlessly. A person indulging in either speech pattern will *talk a blue streak* as long as even one "listener" occasionally nods understanding.

TALK TURKEY

Half a dozen anecdotes seek to explain this expression for speaking plainly. Most of them recount a conversation between a Native American and one or more white settlers. Discussing the division of game bagged in a joint hunt, the native insists that his comrades *talk turkey* and hand over to him the biggest bird shot during the day.

These entertaining frontier stories bypass a skill that was long familiar—and important—to veteran woodsmen.

Many a fellow reared in the woods became an expert turkey caller. That is, he so skillfully imitated sounds made by the big wild birds that some who heard at a distance came within gun range. It was this bona fide turkey talk, not banter at the end of a day's hunt, that spawned our American expression for speaking in a clear and forthright manner.

TAPER OFF

Fire has been associated with worship since prehistoric times, a practice that led to use of candles, or tapers, as symbols of purity and devotion.

Early candles were crude, but worshippers gradually learned how to make long, graceful ones that would burn for hours. Beeswax was and still is employed for many of the finest. Hand-dipped, such a taper is distinctive in shape. Gradually growing smaller, it comes to a definite point at the top.

From the shape of a fine candle, a colorful comparison entered general speech. Anything that diminishes gradually, whether it gives off light or not, is said to *taper off*.

TATTOO

One of the world's greatest explorers, the British navigator Captain James Cook commanded three voyages to the Pacific Ocean and sailed around the world twice. The first European to visit Hawaii and Australia's east coast, he led expeditions in his ship, the *Endeavour*, that resulted in the establishment of colonies throughout the Pacific region by several European nations.

Captain Cook's expedition of 1769 brought him another kind of fame by adding a colorful term to the English language. While spending six weeks in Tahiti, he was intrigued by a strange native custom in which the islanders made gashes in their skin and inserted black pigment. When the wounds healed, they had permanent body markings.

Stumbling over the Tahitian word for this operation, *tatau*, Captain Cook made diary notes about the practice of "tattowing." He was especially interested in the way natives bore the pain of the operation and in the fact that they decorated every part of the body. Today the word *tattoo* names any method of making permanent marks under the skin, though third-millennium operators scorn knives and soot in favor of electric needles and special inks.

TAWDRY

Our word *tawdry*, used as an adjective to describe anything cheap and gaudy in appearance, is a corruption of the name of Saint Audrey, the daughter of an East Anglican king who founded a convent at Ely, England. At the annual autumn fair, nuns from her convent sold a variety of lace known as *Saint Audrey's lace*. Through the years, its quality declined. Common people slurred over their syllables and called it *tawdry's lace*. Eventually, lace and other shoddy articles sold at the fair came to be known simply as *tawdry*.

TEDDY BEAR

It's common knowledge that the *Teddy bear* got its name from President Theodore Roosevelt, but the chain of circumstances that produced the popular toy is not widely known.

Toy bears were first widely advertised in America in 1902, the year Roosevelt went on a big hunt in Mississippi. While in the woods, his dogs found a bear so young that the great hunter refused to shoot it.

Not yet conservation wise, many sportsmen made fun of such sentimental tenderheartedness. For a time Roosevelt was the butt of many jokes. A famous cartoonist sketched Teddy, gun in hand, with his back turned on a small bruin.

People began to associate toys with the incident, so in a matter of months the *Teddy bear* was being featured throughout the nation.

THINKING CAP

Scholars in the Middle Ages wore a distinctive costume. Some of its details varied from one university to another, but two basic pieces were standard—a long black gown and a square-cut cap that fitted tightly against the skull. Clergymen and jurists also wore gowns, so the odd little cap became the symbol of the professional scholar.

Most common folk of the era were illiterate. They had great respect for any man who wore the cap that showed him to possess learning. There was a widespread notion that the cap actually aided its owner to think. Many an idle fellow boasted about what he would do if only he could get a *thinking cap.*

This superstition disappeared long ago. So did the thinking cap, though it left its mark on academic headgear of the third millennium. The expression linked to the costume of early scholars remains in speech, so those wishing to analyze a problem are likely to say that they must put on their *thinking cap* even if they remain bare-headed.

THORN IN THE FLESH

Few sections of the world rival the Holy Land in its number and variety of native prickly plants. At least two hundred species of shrubs and trees of the region are equipped with thorns. Some of them, like the acacia and the buckthorn, make travel difficult where they abound.

In New Testament times, it was a common occurrence to brush against an armored plant. Sometimes a thorn broke off, leaving its point embedded in the flesh. Readers of the letters written by the apostle Paul had no difficulty in understanding his meaning when he described a source of personal vexation as a *thorn in the flesh* (2 Corinthians 12:7).

Even in lands where thorn bushes are not a nuisance to travelers, the phrase is used to describe any persistent problem.

THREE SHEETS TO THE WIND

Especially on New Year's Eve and other festive occasions, you need to keep a close eye on any driver who seems to be *three sheets to the wind.* Whether legally intoxicated or not, anyone who weaves across the road and frequently changes speed is a source of danger.

Sailors in danger of losing their lives created the phrase. For years most people have assumed that *sheets* refers to the ship's sails, but in the old days of sailing a *sheet* was actually a rope, specifically one affixed to the bottom corner of a sail. The sheets, or lines as they're better known, were used to trim the sails to the wind. If they ran loose, the sails would flutter about in the breezes, and soon the ship would be wildly off course.

The rolling and pitching of a poorly rigged ship was much like the actions of a human who has downed too many drinks. Picture sailors on shore leave, staggering back to their boats after a night on the town boozing it up. Put those drunken sailors together with the maritime jargon and you get a pretty clear meaning of *three sheets to the wind,* although the original version of the phrase has been purported to be *three sheets in the wind.*

THRESHOLD

Wheat, oats, rye, and barley were once harvested by hand. Once the grain was gathered, bundles were laced on a hard surface. Then the stalks were *threshed,* or beaten with flails to separate seeds from straw.

Threshing took place in the room with the hardest and flattest floor. Often it was the only room in a hut that was equipped with a plank under the door to keep out vermin.

In Old English, *hold* was widely used to name what we now call wood. Consequently, the beam or plank leading to the threshing floor came to be known as the *threshold.*

Today's point of entrance may have metal or stone underfoot, instead of a doorway plank. When you enter a house, regardless of its construction, a walk across the *threshold* is a reminder that grain is essential to survival of the human race.

THROUGH THE GRAPEVINE

If you receive a message *through the grapevine,* it is likely to be gossip. That is because the newfangled system of communication invented by Samuel F. B. Morse used wires that looked for all the world like vines strung between poles.

Especially during the Civil War, telegraph lines transmitted many wild rumors. Some of them spread so rapidly that soldiers and civilians alike agreed that there must be a *grapevine telegraph* at work in remote regions.

Most battlefield dispatches were true, but some were unfounded. Enough bogus or suspect messages were transmitted that any person-to-person network came to be labeled a *grapevine telegraph,* whose news shouldn't be accepted without question.

THROW COLD WATER

Eighteenth-century doctors attributed insanity to excessive bodily fluids, or "humors." Excitability and nervous tension were associated with this condition, so the object of treatment was to reduce the patient's "mental heat." One prescription was hydrotherapy during which the supposedly demented were stripped naked and showered with cold water for long periods. Thoroughly chilled, the patients sometimes became temporarily docile, and for a time the procedure received great publicity. As a result to *throw cold water* entered common speech as an indication for any action tending to produce apathy.

THROW DOWN THE GAUNTLET

Knights of the age of chivalry were seldom so gallant and noble as they appear in the pages of romances. Many of them were rough, brawling fellows who divided their time between boasting, tippling, and fighting.

As long as opponents used only verbal abuse, there was no certainty that blows would be exchanged. When a man meant business and really wanted to cross swords with a foe, he indicated it by throwing his metal-plated leather glove, or *gauntlet,* to the ground. This constituted his *gage,* or promise of battle.

There are indications that blustering was more common than mortal combat. Still, the custom made sufficient impact to affect general speech. By the time Sir Francis Drake sailed around the globe in the late 1500s, the use of armored gloves had been abandoned, but the expression survives, so to *throw down the gauntlet* still indicates any act of serious challenge.

THROW IN THE TOWEL

Before anyone thought of calling pugilism a science, sluggers went at one another helter-skelter. Even after bare fists were abandoned in favor of light gloves, victory was usually won by beef and brawn rather than skill.

Many a bruised and battered fighter found he could not get to his feet when he heard the signal for a new round to begin. Handlers of such a fellow knew that there was nothing to do but give up. So one of them would toss into the ring an article used to soak up blood— a towel or sponge.

Modern boxing is replete with rules designed to outlaw the brutality of the past. Even the lingo of the ring has become larger and richer. But in an era of instant replays for television, a person forced to give up at ringside or anywhere else is still said to *throw in the towel.*

THUNDERSTRUCK

As late as the seventeenth century, a few common folk knew that thunder is the noise that follows a lightning flash. Many people caught outdoors in a violent storm feared thunderbolts almost as much as lightning.

Fear and trembling were so common during storms that these atmospheric disturbances were linked with any state of acute terror.

A seventeenth-century poet described a love-shaken youth as being so "thunder-stroken" that he was "void of sense."

Since the time of Benjamin Franklin, we have known that thunder is never dangerous. But earlier notions about it are firmly embedded in language. As a result, a person who seems speechless from surprise or fear is likely to be described as being *thunderstruck*.

TIE THE KNOT

In some parts of the world, until recent times, the taking of a wife did not necessarily involve going before a clergyman, priest, or civic official. Especially in the East, the family patriarch performed most religious and civil functions.

In many places, the patriarch performed the marriage ceremony quite simply. He would lay his hands on the bride and groom in blessing, then knot together their sleeves or two corners of their flowing robes. No vows were exchanged; to *tie the knot* symbolized the permanence of the union.

TO A T

Ancient Hebrew scribes did much of their writing with little brushes. Numerous letters were distinguished from one another only by patterns of minute brush marks. Because of their shape, these marks were commonly known as *horns*. It became proverbial that a careful scribe copied material exactly—that is, *to a horn*.

A reference to these little marks is included in the New Testament (Matthew 5:18). When John Wycliffe issued his famous English translation of the Bible in 1382, he referred to the horn as a "titil." This word was later spelled *tittle*, and *to a tittle* became a proverbial expression for scrupulous care. Abbreviated in common usage, the phrase lives on. Now when something is done with precision, it is said to be done *to a T*.

TOE THE MARK

Unlike their American cousins, entrants in a properly British foot race of the nineteenth century were not required to come up to scratch. Instead, the official solemnly intoned: "Gentlemen, toe your marks!"

Naturally, every contestant wanted to be as far forward as possible at the moment a race began. But an entrant who pushed toes a trifle past the starting mark was thrown out of the contest, with no second chance.

It took both practice and careful attention to *toe the mark* without going past it. Hence the English sporting term came to be used on both sides of the Atlantic to mean meeting a standard or abiding by a rule.

TOMBOY

A *tomboy*, says oral tradition, gets her name from the fact that she is a changeling, or a female who has been given the appearance of a male. Though the idea is plausible enough, it has no basis in fact.

Tom and Jerry cartoons are modern, but the characters that gave them their names are not. During the reign of England's King George IV, his subjects became enamored with an 1821 volume about *Life in London*. It featured the antics of Tom and Jerry—who were as zany as today's cartoon characters.

Popular talk about goings-on of the fellows who were credited with making London life lively was enhanced by using *Tom* to denote maleness, as in *tomcat*. With its origins forgotten, the label attached to a young female whose looks are as deceptive as were the actions of early Toms—real or imaginary.

TONE DOWN

During the last quarter of the eighteenth century, a group of rebels defied the conventions of art. Led by J. M. W. Turner, a group of English painters began using a wide variety of vivid colors. Inevitably, a reaction followed, and early nineteenth-century artists returned to the use of more subdued tones.

As the trend vanished, the owner of a bright canvas often covered it with a coat of oil or varnish in order to soften its tones. Many second-rate paintings, and a few fine ones, were treated in this fashion. Hence to *tone down* became a standard term indicating any move toward moderation or reduction of extremes.

TONIC

Though numerous types of illness are highly specific, it's not easy to define a state of good health. Physicians of a few centuries ago considered such well-being to rest largely upon proper firmness or tension in organs and tissues. So *tone* was used to designate any general condition. Never very precise, *tone* was a major medical term during much of the seventeenth and eighteenth centuries.

Anything that fostered the rather nebulous *tone of the body* came to be called a *tonic* or *tone enhancer*. Fresh air was high on the list of such agencies. Later, iron compounds came into general use as tonic bitters. Though many experts now discount the importance of bodily tension as an index to health, any medicine designed to aid general welfare rather than a precise condition is still known as a *tonic*.

TOUCH WITH A TEN-FOOT POLE

When a person is unwilling to become involved in a project, he is likely to say he won't *touch it with a ten-foot pole*. It seems odd that we should always specify that length rather than sometimes referring to a nine- or a twelve-foot piece.

Reasons for stipulating a ten-foot pole are buried deep in American history. Pioneers who pushed into frontier country learned to make good use of rivers, swamps, and lakes. Special pole boats with flat bottoms were used for hauling everything from household goods to bales of cotton. Deep water was dangerous; currents could snatch a clumsy pole boat and dash it against rocks or throw it upon a mud bar. So it became standard practice for boatmen to cut their poles just ten feet long then use them to measure depth as well as to push.

In river towns and farm communities alike, a person wishing to avoid a situation would say he wouldn't *touch it with a ten-foot pole* of a river man. The expression became so firmly fixed that it survives long after modern vessels put pole boats out of business.

TOUGH ROW TO HOE

Europeans who came to America as colonists found the new country to have a great deal of level, fertile farmland, but some settlers pushed away from the coast into the foothills of the Appalachian Mountains. A pioneer typically would build his cabin in a remote spot where plowing was difficult because of the terrain.

Matters were further complicated by the scarcity of work animals and gear. Hence, the backwoods farmer in such regions as the Kentucky border leaned heavily on hand labor. These farmers usually had large families, and every member was expected to wield a hoe many days each year.

Monotonous at best, such labor was likely to become very distasteful toward the close of a warm day. A youngster working against his will was likely to beg relief and complain that he had a *tough row to hoe*. Hence, the phrase came to stand for any difficult or unpleasant task.

TOWERING AMBITION

A passionate yearning for success is frequently described as *towering ambition*. This expression owes its place in the language to the medieval passion for falconry. Many types of killer hawks were bred in captivity then trained to capture game birds. A falcon's ability as a hunter was partly measured by the speed with which he gained enough altitude to swoop down on his prey. Because watchtowers were the tallest buildings of the period, the hawk that flew high in the air was said to *tower*.

Many falcons were haughty and cruel and had little affection for anyone, not even the trainer who fed them daily. Such a bird's high towering in search of prey was not unlike the upward sweep of an ambitious person. So a man dominated by desire for success was said to *tower*. With the decline of falconry the term was modified in popular speech, so that *towering ambition* came to stand for any ambition that is a controlling force in life.

TRUE BLUE

Cloth, made by hand, was long dyed in the household. Berries, bark, and a few blossoms yielded most of the coloring matter used. Even when synthetic dyes came on the market, most of them were of inferior quality. Consequently, cloth often faded after a few washings.

Artisans of Coventry, England, discovered and kept secret a formula for the manufacture of a blue dye of superior quality. This Coventry blue—or *true blue*—remained bright after many washings.

For generations, *true blue* was absolutely the best that could be bought. From chatter of those who labored over dye vats and washtubs, the term entered general speech to stand for faithfulness and reliability of every sort.

TWO TO TANGO

No one is sure how a Latin American dance first zoomed to popularity in the U.S. Probably adapted from the beat of tribal drums in Africa, the tango in two-quarter and four-quarter time was found to be especially exhilarating by some who experimented with it.

Many dances lend themselves to solo exhibitions. Not so the

tango. This aspect of what was once a novel form of entertainment was emphasized in a popular song of the 1930s that stressed "It takes two to tango!"

That made a vivid and emphatic way of saying that some activities require two participants. So the dance-floor expression originally came into wide use as a response to accusations of sexual misconduct. Today it has become a defense for any situation in which no one assumes full blame.

UMPIRE

Rude athletic contests were in great vogue among rough tribesmen who swarmed through western Europe after the fall of the Roman Empire. Since they were violent and often bloody, such games were staged between teams matched as evenly as possible. Every man on one side had a specific opponent on the other.

Disputes sometimes arose. In order to settle them with a minimum of violence, a nonparticipant was chosen as judge. Since he wasn't matched against an opponent, the judge was treated as an odd man—that is, not paired or *unpaired.* Crossing the Channel with the Normans who conquered Britain in the eleventh century, the old sporting term emerged into modern speech as *umpire.*

UNCLE TOM

Angry at the continued tolerance of slavery in the United States, Harriet Beecher Stowe wrote the novel *Uncle Tom's Cabin* that depicted the system at its worst. When it appeared in book form in 1852, it created a national sensation.

One of her major characters didn't want trouble and was inclined to seek peace at any price. Even when he was sold by his owner, Uncle Tom made no outcry—he simply resigned himself to the hand of Providence.

Few novels have affected life so greatly as did *Uncle Tom's Cabin.*

Few characters have aroused more controversy than the slave who accepted his fate without questioning. Today, an *Uncle Tom* is an African-American male who behaves deferentially to whites. The term, of course, is in the highest order of insults.

UNDERDOG

Settlers who were pioneers on the American frontier were usually ready for a brawl. Many of them enjoyed fighting among themselves. Practically all made quite a sport of setting lean hounds upon one another.

Dog fighting has one significant factor in common with wrestling by humans. In both cases, it is a decided disadvantage to be on the bottom. That was notably the case in a backwoods dog-fight. When one animal got the other down and started for its throat, some bystander had to intervene in order to save the life of the dog underneath.

Regular reference to losses by canines on the bottom caused the title of *Underdog* to be bestowed on any contestant—two-legged or four-legged—judged likely to be at a disadvantage in a struggle.

UP A CREEK

Most rivers of England and Europe are fairly small. Even before the advent of modern highways, the rivulets, or creeks, of these regions posed a few obstacles to travelers.

Settlers in the New World found a different situation. Rivers such as the Ohio, the Mississippi, and the Missouri were so mighty that even large streams seemed to be creeks by comparison.

A hunter or explorer sometimes tried to cross at an untried spot. If he misjudged the speed or depth of water, he might be trapped up the creek until rescued.

Modern bridges have eliminated most hazards posed by flowing water. Yet a person whose feet are not wet may suddenly be caught *up a creek*—stuck in a dilemma from which it is hard to escape without help.

UP TO SNUFF

During the seventeenth century, Europeans developed a great passion for finely powdered tobacco, or *snuff*. So many Englishmen became fond of it that it was in nearly universal use among them. Users customarily grated tobacco on the spot. For this purpose, they carried around boxes that held coarse tobacco, with spoons and graters attached.

Advent of commercially ground mixtures brought an end to the use of individual snuff graters. But connoisseurs continue to pride themselves on being able to distinguish good from poor. A sharp fellow, not easily deceived, was said to be *up to snuff*—or able to discern quality at a sniff.

In popular speech, a negative form of the phrase came to label a simpleton or a gullible fellow. At first the new term was used literally. One derided as *not up to snuff* was considered an amateur at judging powdered tobacco. Soon the expression expanded and became a label of ridicule for any person or product considered to be less than discerning or below standard.

UPSHOT

Villagers of medieval Britain took archery seriously. Big matches were gala affairs that affected the social standing of participants. Many were conducted like modern sporting events; the winner of a given round moved up to the next.

Competitors were often so closely matched that the last shot of a round determined its outcome. In such circumstances a single arrow caused one man to drop out, another to move up toward a new opponent.

A shot that propelled an archer upward is competition came to be known as an *upshot*. Use of the sporting word by Shakespeare and Milton caused it to enter general speech. We employ it to name any type of result or conclusion, no matter how remote from activities on the village green.

VIRUS

When scientists first isolated a minute parasitic structure that caused serious illness, they called it a *virus,* which is Latin for "poison." Unable to live in isolation, a virus inside a suitable host organism such as a human body can reproduce with incredible speed.

When hackers and other computer enthusiasts discovered how to insert a small self-replicating program into a larger "host" program, the name was obvious: electronic *virus.* Such a set of data cannot travel or survive by itself but thrives as a parasite when it gets inside a computer. Like a submicroscopic particle of biochemistry, a computer *virus* can do great damage to any host in which it lodges, whether sent there deliberately or picked up accidentally.

WASH ONE'S HANDS

Modern drama was born in the church where plays and interludes based upon the Bible were used for centuries as a means of instruction of illiterate parishioners. Strolling bands of minstrels also performed biblical dramas at street fairs and had a great impact upon popular thought and speech.

A favorite scene was the enactment of Jesus' trial before Pilate. There were few props to make the background seem realistic, but it was customary to bring in a basin of water. Pilate then washed his hands as he denied responsibility for the death sentence. This bit of stage play made a great hit with audiences. As a result, to *wash one's hands* of a matter came into general use as an expression denying accountability.

WELL-HEELED

If someone comments that you are *well-heeled*, say "Thank you," regardless of the amount of money in your pocket. This compliment stems from cockfights of the Middle Ages.

Birds fought to the death. Some with good bloodlines were handicapped by short spurs. Owners learned to equip such a cock with a metal spur, or gaff. Strapped close to the heel of a fighter, it was even more lethal than a natural growth of bone and cartilage.

A bird equipped with a pair of gaffs was well-heeled indeed— it was armed for quick victory. Since plenty of money is a major weapon in a business or industrial fight, anyone with ample resources came to bear the label of a fighting cock wearing gaffs.

WET BEHIND THE EARS

A person *wet behind the ears* barely qualifies as a beginner. Compared with such a neophyte, a tenderfoot or greenhorn is an old pro.

Many newly born animals, wet from liquids in the womb, are slow to become fully dry. Some places, especially the indentation behind the ears, take the longest because they are not exposed to the air. The fur of animals like kittens and colts holds moisture and stays damp until they are active.

A youth or an adult who knows absolutely nothing about a planned undertaking is a helpless infant in that field, or *wet behind the ears*.

WHAMMY

Strange as it may seem, the world of entertainment gave us *whammy* as a name for a potent spell or curse. Al Capp, creator of *Li'l Abner*, popularized this expression.

Millions of readers who regularly laughed at the goings-on in Dogpatch came to know each character in the strip.

One of Capp's creature characterizations knew enough about Native-American lore to paralyze with a stare—a fearful glance that the cartoonist called a *whammy*. Once the term became familiar to readers, it was not unusual to see someone receive a double-whammy—a glance so potent that its recipient was frozen in his or her tracks.

WHIPPERSNAPPER

No doubt you have noticed that any person who is called *whippersnapper* is either a juvenile or a learner who is barely dry behind the ears. The full title addressed to such a person by the boss or used out of hearing is likely to be *young whippersnapper*.

One of the easiest skills learned by a greenhorn cowboy is that of snapping a black-snake whip. Decades ago, lots of fellows who could not bulldog a steer or rope a maverick prided themselves on being able to strut into a village while calling attention to themselves by snapping their whips.

Only neophytes, young fellows who did not even tote guns, followed this practice. But it was common enough to lead folk who never saw a trail herd's dust to adopt *whippersnapper* as just the right label for any brash but unskilled beginner.

WHISTLE BLOWER

A *whistle blower* who is interviewed for the television shows *60 Minutes* or *20/20* is likely to get results. Nuclear plants, suppliers of military hardware, and manufacturers of chemicals are prime targets. The whistles of police are still heard in some cities. Their impact may have had a little influence in the formation of the modern title for an informer. However, action on the basketball court has been much more significant.

Watch a game in the NCAA finals and count the number of

times an official blows a whistle. Most of the time, the sound of an official's whistle means "Stop instantly!"—which is the goal of the industrial or environmental whistle blower as well.

The main object of *whistle blowers* is to stop illegal action and infringement on the rules of the game.

WHITE ELEPHANT

One of the rarest creatures in Thailand, once known as Siam, is the albino elephant. For centuries it was regarded as sacred. Virtually all white elephants were claimed by some member of a royal family, who could afford to keep it on exhibition for admiration of visitors.

When an ordinary citizen incurred the wrath of a blue blood, it wasn't necessary to find a way to squeeze money out of him in order to hurt him. Instead, the offender received the gift of a white elephant that he had to feed and could not work. Eventually, the British coined the phrase *white elephant* to mean a valuable item that is unwanted but cannot be given away.

WOODEN NICKELS

Early Yankee tradesmen showed the same skill and tenacity that has led their descendants to be credited with the ability to sell refrigerators to the Eskimos. Some of them cracked jokes about peddling wooden substitutes for good merchandise, while others did it when they could. In 1832 the *Boston Transcript* warned: "We recently read of wooden hams in some parts of the west neatly sewed up in canvass, said to have their origin with the same ingenious people who invented wooden nutmegs."

It was believed that some fellows, unwilling to do an honest day's work, would go to the trouble of making wooden nickels. That was considerable trouble to go to for such a small amount of money. Whether or not any phony nickels were ever made, it became proverbial that greenhorns had better watch out for them. The jocular warning "Don't take any *wooden nickels!*" remains in speech as a memorial to the ingenuity of swindlers, the imagination of tale spinners, or both.

WRONG SIDE OF THE BED

Nearly everything we use is shaped for right-handed people. Even a dexterous southpaw may sometimes seem awkward. As a result, among the ancients the left side of the body or anything else was considered to be sinister—mysterious and dangerous, maybe even evil.

Old-time innkeepers often pushed the left sides of the bed against the walls so that guests could get up only on the right side.

Many who sleep in king- or queen-size modern beds attach little or no importance to the side that is used. But when a person shows unusual irritability or clumsiness, it may be called the result of having started the day by getting up on *the wrong side of the bed.*

X (FOR KISS)

Our custom of putting *X*s at the end of letters to symbolize kisses grew out of medieval legal practices. In order to indicate good faith and honesty, the sign of Saint Andrew was placed after the signature on all important documents. This sign is quite like the letter *X*.

Contracts and agreements were not considered binding until each signer added Saint Andrew's cross after his name. Then he was required to kiss it to guarantee the faithful performance of his obligations.

Over the centuries, the origin of the ceremony was forgotten. People associated *X* with the kiss instead of the pledge of good faith, and the modern custom was born.

BIBLIOGRAPHY

More detailed information concerning most words and phrases in *Casual Lex* may be found in one or more of the following volumes. For the roots of standard English and American words, consult etymological dictionaries. By all odds, the most valuable single work in print is the revised edition of the *Oxford English Dictionary*. Yet even this monumental work of scholarship omits numerous contemporary expressions that are American, rather than British.

Words and phrases not yet accepted as standard speech are treated in volumes dealing with slang. Many of these, but not all, appear in the *American Heritage Dictionary*, where brief hints concerning their origins are often included.

Adams, James T., *Dictionary of American History*. 7 vols. New York: Scribner's, 1940.

Alsager, Christian M., ed., *Dictionary of Business Terms*. Chicago: Callaghan, 1932.

American Heritage Dictionary. 4th ed. New York: Dell Pub., 2001.

American Heritage Dictionary of the English Language. 4th. ed. Boston: Houghton Mifflin, 2000.

Ammer, Christine, *Have a Nice Day—No Problem!: A Dictionary of Cliches*. New York: Dutton, 1992.

Annual Register, The. London: Longmans, Green, 1670–1985.

Ayto, John, *Dictionary of Word Origins*. New York: Arcade, 1990.

Barrere, A., *Argot and Slang*. London: Whittaker, 1887.

Bartlett, John R., *Dictionary of Americanisms*. Boston: Little, Brown, 1877.

_____, ed., *Familiar Quotations*. 17th ed. Boston: Little, Brown, 2002.

Berliner, Barbara, *The Book of Answers*. New York: Prentice Hall, 1990.

Berrey, Lester V. and Melvin Van Den Bark, *The American Thesaurus of Slang*. New York: Crowell, 1962.

Blunt, John H., *Dictionary of Sects*. London: Rivingtons, 1874.

Bodmer, Frederick, *The Loom of Language*. New York: Norton, 1944.

Bombaugh, C. C., *Facts and Fancies for the Curious*. Philadelphia: Lippincott, 1905.

Brand-Ellis, John, *Popular Antiquities of Great Britain*. 2 vols. London: Reeves and Turner, 1905.

Brewer, E. C., *A Dictionary of Miracles*. Philadelphia: Lippincott, 1934.

_____, *Dictionary of Phrase and Fable*. New York: Harper, 1953.

_____, *The Historic Note-Book*. Philadelphia: Lippincott, 1891.

_____, *The Reader's Handbook*. Philadelphia: Lippincott, 1904.

Chambers, Robert, *The Book of Days*. 2 vols. London: Chambers, 1869.

_____, *The Book of Days*. Philadelphia: Lippincott, 1899.

Cambridge History of English Literature, The. 15 vols. Cambridge: Cambridge University Press, 1907–33.

Cambridge History of the British Empire, The. 7 vols. Cambridge: Cambridge University Press, 1919–40.

Cambridge Medieval History, The New. 7 vols. Cambridge: Cambridge University Press, 1995–2005.

Cambridge Modern History, The New. 14 vols. Cambridge: Cambridge University Press, 1957–2000.

Catholic Encyclopedia, The. 15 vols. New York: Universal Knowledge Foundation, 1912.

Chapman, Robert L., ed. *The Dictionary of American Slang*. 3d ed. New York: Harper Collins, 1995.

De Vore, Nicholas, ed., *Encyclopedia of Astrology*. New York: Philosophical Library, 1947.

Dickson, Paul, *Dickson's Word Treasury*. New York: John Wiley and Sons, 1992.

Dictionary of National Biography. 66 vols. London: Oxford University Press, 1952.

Dixon, James M., ed., *Dictionary of Idiomatic English Phrases*. London: Nelson, 1891.

Encarta World English Dictionary. New York: Saint Martin's, 1999.

Espy, Willard R., *Thou Improper, Thou Uncommon Noun*. New York: Clarkson Potter, 1972.

Evans, Bergan and Cornelia, *A Dictionary of Contemporary American Usage*. New York: Random House, 1957.

Farmer, John S. and W. E. Henley, *Slang and Its Analogues*. 7 vols. New Hyde Park: University Press, 1966.

——————, *Slang and Its Analogues*. New York: Arno reprint, 1970.

Flexner, Stuart B., *I Hear America Talking*. New York: Van Nostrand, 1976.

——————, *Listening to America*. New York: Simon and Schuster, 1982.

Funk, Charles E., *Heavens to Betsy!* New York: Warner Paperback Library, 1972.

——————, *Hereby Hangs a Tale*. New York: Warner Paperback Library, 1972.

——————, *A Hog on Ice*. New York: Warner Paperback Library, 1972.

——————, *Horsefeathers*. New York: Warner Paperback Library, 1972.

Goldin, Hyman E., *Dictionary of American Underworld Lingo*. New York: Twayne, 1950.

Granville, Wilfred, *A Dictionary of Sailors' Slang*. London: Deutsch, 1962.

Grun, Bernard, *The Timetables of History*. New York: Simon and Schuster, 1975.

Hargrove, Basil, *Origins and Meanings of Popular Phrases and Names*. Philadelphia: Lippincott, 1925.

Hastings, James, ed., *Encyclopedia of Religion and Ethics*. 13 vols. New York: Scribner's, 1928.

Hendrickson, Robert, *The Dictionary of Eponyms*. New York: Dorset, 1972.

Hollander, Zander, ed., *The Encyclopedia of Sports Talk*. New York: Corwin, 1976.

Holt, Alfred H., *Phrase and Word Origins*. New York: Dover, 1961.

Holt, Alfred M., *Phrase Origins*. New York: Crowell, 1936.

Hunt, Cecil, *Word Origins: The Romance of Language*. New York: Philosophical, 1949.

Lass, A. H.; Kiremidjian, D.; and Goldstein, R. M., *Dictionary of Classical, Biblical, and Literary Allusions*. New York: Facts on File Publications, 1987.

Little, Charles E., ed., *Cyclopedia of Classified Dates*. New York: Funk and Wagnalls, 1900.

McEwen, William A., *Encyclopedia of Nautical Knowledge*. Cambridge, Md.: Cornell Maritime Press, 1953.

Manser, Martin, *Get to the Roots: A Dictionary of Word and Phrase Origins*. New York: Avon, 1990.

Matthews, Mitford M., ed., *Dictionary of Americanisms*. 2 vols. Chicago: University of Chicago Press, 1951.

Mencken, H. L., *The American Language*. 3 vols. New York: Knopf, 1936–48.

Menke, Frank G., ed., *New Encyclopedia of Sports*. New York: Barnes, 1947.

Quinron, Michaels, *World Wide Words*, 1996–2005, as viewed on www.worldwidewords.org.

Morris, Richard B., ed., *Encyclopedia of American History*. New York: Harper, 1953.

Morris, William and Mary Morris, *Dictionary of Word and Phrase Origins*. 2d ed. New York: Harper Collins Publishers, 1988.

Munn, Glenn G., ed., *Encyclopedia of Banking and Finance*. Cambridge, Mass.: Bankers' Publishing Co. 1949.

Notes and Queries. London: Bell, 1810–1990.

Onions, C. T., ed., *The Oxford Dictionary of English Etymology*. Oxford: Clarendon, 1966.

Oxford English Dictionary. 10 vols. Oxford: Oxford University Press, 1888–1935.

Oxford English Dictionary. Supp. 4 vols. R. W. Burchfield, ed. Oxford: Oxford University Press, 1987.

Oxford English Dictionary. 2d ed. 20 vols. J. A. Simpson and Edmund S. Weiner, eds. Oxford: Oxford University Press, 1989.

Partridge, Eric, ed., *Dictionary of Cliches*. New York: Macmillan, 1940.

_____, ed., *Dictionary of Slang*. New York: Macmillan, 1938.

Partridge, Eric, *A Dictionary of Slang and Unconventional English*. New York: Macmillan, 1961.

_____, *Origins*. New York: Macmillan, 1966.

_____, *Origins*. New York: Greenwich House, 1983.

_____, *A Dictionary of the Underworld*. New York: Macmillan, 1961.

_____, *Name Into Word*. London: Routledge, 1949.

Radford, Edwin M., ed., *Encyclopedia of Superstitions*. New York: Philosophical Library, 1949.

Roback, Aaron A., *Dictionary of International Slurs*. Cambridge: Sci-Art, 1944.

Runes, Dagobert D., ed., *Encyclopedia of the Arts*. New York: Philosophical Library, 1945.

Seligman, Edwin R. A., ed., *Encyclopedia of the Social Sciences*. 15 vols. New York: Macmillan, 1930–35.

Seyffert, Oskar, ed., *Dictionary of Classical Antiquities*. New York: Macmillan, 1891.

Shipley, Joseph T., *Dictionary of Word Origins*. New York: Littlefield, 1967.

Skeat, Walter W., *An Etymological Dictionary of the English Language*. Rev. ed. London: Oxford University Press, 1963.

Skeat, Walter W., ed., *Concise Etymological Dictionary*. Oxford: Clarendon, 1948.

Smith, Benjamin E., ed., *Century Cyclopedia of Names*. New York: Century, 1914.

_____, ed., *The Home Book of Proverbs, Maxims, and Familiar Phrases*. New York: Macmillan, 1948.

_____, ed., *Home Book of Quotations*. New York: Dodd, Mead, 1947.

Sorel, Nancy C., *Word People*. New York: American Heritage Press, 1970.

Thomas, Joseph, *Dictionary of Biography and Mythology*. Philadelphia: Lippincott, 1930.

Webster's New World Dictionary of American English. 3d coll. ed. New York: Prentice Hall, 1994.

Webster's New International Dictionary of the English Language. Springfield, Mass.: Merriam, 1947.

Weekley, Ernest, *Concise Etymological Dictionary of Modern English*. New York: Dutton, 1924.

_____, *The Romance of Names*. London: Murray, 1922.

_____, *The Romance of Words*. New York: Dover, 1961.

_____, *Surnames*. London: Murray, 1917.

Wentworth, Harold and Stuart B. Flexner, *Dictionary of American Slang*. New York: Crowell, 1934.

Weseen, Maurice H., ed., *Dictionary of American Slang*. New York: Crowell, 1934.

Wright, James, ed., *English Dialect Dictionary*. 6 vols. London: Oxford University Press, 1924.

ABOUT THE AUTHOR

Webb Garrison, formerly associate dean of Emory University and president of McKendree College, was the author of more than 55 books, including *Civil War Curiosities* and *Civil War Trivia and Fact Book*. Before his death in the summer of 2000, Garrison lived in Lake Junaluska, North Carolina.